Best Hikes Near
Washington, D.C.

BILL AND MARY BURNHAM

FALCONGUIDES

GUILFORD, CONNECTICUT
HELENA, MONTANA

AN IMPRINT OF GLOBE PEQUOT PRESS

To Jenny, Mike, and the kids

To buy books in quantity for corporate use
or incentives, call **(800) 962–0973**
or e-mail **premiums@GlobePequot.com**.

FALCONGUIDES®

Copyright © 2010 by Morris Book Publishing, LLC

FalconGuides is an imprint of Globe Pequot Press.
Falcon, FalconGuides, and Outfit Your Mind are registered trademarks of Morris Book Publishing, LLC.

Interior photos: Mary and Bill Burnham unless otherwise credited
Art on page i © Shutterstock
Project editor: Julie Marsh
Text design: Sheryl P. Kober
Layout artist: Maggie Peterson
Maps: Design Maps Inc. © Morris Book Publishing, LLC

Library of Congress Cataloging-in-Publication Data

Burnham, Mary (Mary K.)
  Best hikes near Washington, D.C. / Mary and Bill Burnham.
    p. cm. — (Falconguides)
  ISBN 978-0-7627-4695-8
  1. Hiking—Washington Region—Guidebooks. 2. Washington Region—Guidebooks. I. Burnham, Bill, 1969- II. Title.
  GV199.42.W17B87 2010
  796.510975—dc22
                                                                        2009039358

Printed in China
10 9 8 7 6 5 4 3 2 1

Contents

Washington, D.C., Overview

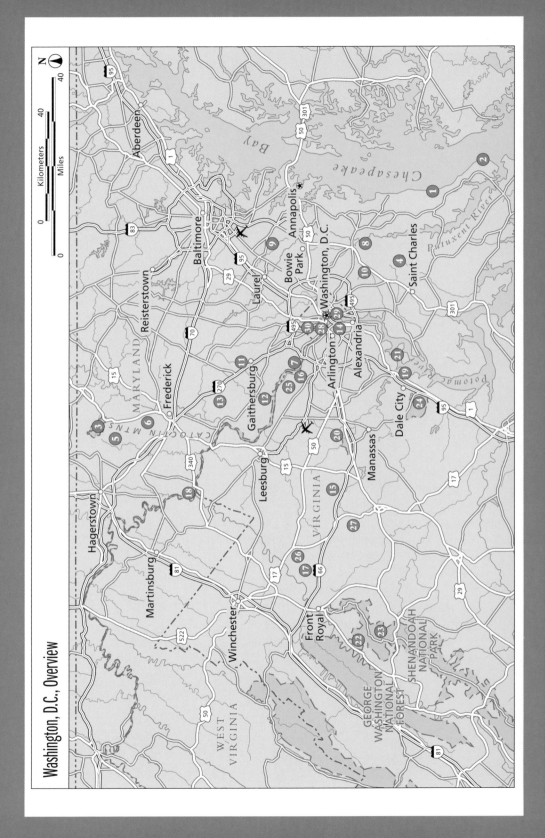

Author with nephew Gregory Nardacci, the next generation

HELP US KEEP THIS GUIDE UP TO DATE

Every effort has been made by the authors and editors to make this guide as accurate and useful as possible. However, many things can change after a guide is published—trails are rerouted, regulations change, techniques evolve, facilities come under new management, and so on.

We would appreciate hearing from you concerning your experiences with this guide and how you feel it could be improved and kept up to date. While we may not be able to respond to all comments and suggestions, we'll take them to heart, and we'll also make certain to share them with the authors. Please send your comments and suggestions to the following address:

GPP
Reader Response/Editorial Department
P.O. Box 480
Guilford, CT 06437

Or you may e-mail us at: editorial@globepequot.com

Thanks for your input, and happy trails!

Introduction

Mary and I relish this opportunity to share with you our favorite hikes in metro Washington, D.C., the Blue Ridge, and the Coastal Plain with *Best Hikes Near Washington, D.C.*, our first hiking guide since *Hiking Virginia*. Although we've been hiking Virginia and Maryland for more than a decade, it was with fresh eyes that we explored freshwater marshes along the Patuxent River at Jug Bay and felt the rough sandstone beneath our hands and knees on Catoctin Mountain Park. We absorbed the majesty of a 96-foot free-falling waterfall in Shenandoah National Park and enjoyed the discovery of new places like the American Chestnut Land Trust Preserve.

We also savored the quiet scenes: hiking through the muggy morning mist the day after a heavy rain, our ears ringing with the shrill call of spring peepers; studying wildflowers; enjoying the company of trail friends; learning how locals find the treasured morel mushrooms. All these experiences and more helped us press on in discovering and presenting to you the very best day hiking in and around Washington, D.C.

The diversity of terrain, climate, culture, and environment encompassed in this compact region is mind-boggling. The Chesapeake Bay laps at your feet at Calvert Cliffs State Park in Maryland. (These high cliffs glistened with such intensity

Jogger on the Mount Vernon Trail (Hike 14)

on a June day in 1608 that they served as a beacon for Capt. John Smith and his crew of fifteen men circumnavigating the Chesapeake Bay.) Barely 30 miles west as the crow flies, you land in the Zekiah Swamp in Charles County, Maryland, whose wet, mysterious woodlands briefly sheltered fugitive John Wilkes Booth, a man shunned after he assassinated President Abraham Lincoln in 1865.

Continue west another 30 miles, across the Potomac River separating Maryland and Virginia, to find Prince William Forest Park in Prince William County, Virginia. Here, the Quantico and South Fork Quantico Creeks cascade over the "fall line," the geologic cleft that demarks the Coastal Plain from the Piedmont. Waterfalls cascade over one another on these creeks, as they do at places along the fall line north and south, at Great Falls of the Potomac and elsewhere.

Another 30 miles west finds the hiker in the foothills of the Blue Ridge. Small "hills" of resistant quartzite bedrock have withstood the weathering of time. At Bull Run Mountains near Thoroughfare Gap, and Wildcat Mountain near Warrensburg, a hike through the woodlands foreshadows the rugged mountain terrain that awaits just another 30 miles west in the Blue Ridge and Catoctin Mountain regions.

By straight line, our trip of 120 miles spans the Bay to the Blue Ridge. In between, we've left no stone unturned to document only the very best of the hikes found here.

Great Falls

WEATHER

Befitting its geographic diversity, weather in metro Washington, D.C., and outlying areas varies to the extremes. On a mild winter day along the Patuxent River in Calvert County, it may be snowing in Shenandoah National Park. Temperatures fluctuate throughout the year from midsummer highs of 90°F or more to winter low temperatures in the teens. Generally speaking, hikers will find coastal areas are tempered by Chesapeake Bay breezes, while higher elevations west and north swing from extreme high to extreme low temperatures depending on the season. It's not an exaggeration to state that in a matter of an hour, you can drive from shorts weather in the Piedmont to sweater weather in the Blue Ridge.

The best months for comfortable hiking temperatures are the "shoulder" seasons of spring and fall. Summertime becomes extremely humid; in spring and summer, fast-moving and often violent storms can alter your hiking plans within minutes. In Prince William Forest Park, a springtime storm altered the course of the Quantico River and its South Branch to such an extent that floodplains, once lush with grass, small shrubs, and skinny trees, were scoured clean by water that rose several feet in a matter of an hour. Tree trunks as thick as a bridge piling were tossed about like toothpicks. One need not have witnessed it in person, but only walk the trails in its aftermath, to gain a new appreciation for weather's powerful impact on the environment.

The author pauses at the Jefferson Memorial (Hike 29).

Many try to escape the height of city heat by heading to higher elevations or by seeking out coastal breezes. Or, you can pass up the hot sun and concrete of the capital by slipping into Rock Creek Park or its neighboring stream valley parks around Georgetown. Winter hiking on a cloudless blue day brings the reward of uncrowded trails and unobstructed views through a leafless forest. Summer thunderstorms with dangerous lightning are quick moving and dramatic, while fall might bring a tropical storm. Flash flooding may occur on some trails and along streambeds. Always check the NOAA weather reports on a weather-band radio or online before heading out.

FLORA AND FAUNA

Mid-Atlantic forests are primarily broadleaf, deciduous trees. In moist pockets below 4,500 feet elevation, the Appalachian cove forest holds more than twenty species of trees: beech, sugar maple, and yellow poplar noticeable among these. Stands of eastern hemlock once made for impressive viewing; however, damage from the invasive woolly adelgid is now widespread. Evidence of its work is especially striking in Shenandoah National Park, where entire stands of hemlock are defoliated and dying. Even so, quiet, cool pockets of this venerable evergreen may still be found along isolated mountain streams.

The Appalachian oak-hickory forest rises to dominance with the Blue Ridge. Hickory is the successor of the American chestnut. In the early twentieth century,

White-tailed deer are common sightings on woodland trails.

it was estimated one of every four trees in the Appalachians was a chestnut. Today, few grow taller than 6 feet before succumbing to the chestnut blight.

Virginia's Piedmont has traditionally supported agriculture. By the twentieth century, generations of farming left large swaths of barren land. Where forest returned, they are primarily bland white oak and Virginia and loblolly pine. In Virginia state and national forests, oak and poplar are managed for harvest. Willow oak, river birch, hickory, and ash grow as well. Turkey, fox, deer, raccoon, and squirrel populate these pockets of rejuvenated woodlands.

Grasses, saltmeadow hay, and hearty shrubs such as wax myrtle populate coastal fringes. These are some of the most resilient plants in the world, able to withstand harsh winds and saltwater conditions. Inland from the beaches and dunes, lagoons mix a daily tidal wash with mainland runoff. Fish spawn here, and crustaceans such as fiddler crab live out early years on a nutrient-rich diet. On the mainland, forests of pines and oak typify the flat coastal region. In swampy areas, bald cypress and live oak are often draped with Spanish moss.

Violet

The forest understory provides the hiker with a seasonal palette of color. White dogwood and delicate pink redbud come before trees leaf out in early spring. Thousands of cherry trees bloom pale pink on the National Mall in April. Throughout the forest, the ubiquitous mountain laurel blooms in May, and its cousin the rhododendron in July.

Don't forget to look down: Wildflowers are profuse throughout the region in spring, from common purple violets, spring beauties, and white toothwort to the more rare Turks cap lily. G. Richard Thompson Wildlife Management Area is thought to hold the largest North American population of large-flowered trillium, a white tripetal flower. Beginning in late winter/early spring, look for naturalized daffodils around old homesteads. Since they don't grow naturally, wherever you see these cheerful harbingers of spring, you'll undoubtedly find the remains of a home foundation, a rock wall, a fence, or a well nearby.

Deer have rebounded from overhunting and habitat destruction of a century ago to rank as almost a nuisance in some areas. Black bear are found in the Blue Ridge and are quite common sightings in Shenandoah National Park. A hiker's footsteps may flush turkey or grouse. Raccoon are primarily nocturnal animals and are scavengers, so be mindful of dropping any trash or food crumbs. Bobcat and coyote are found throughout the region, but generally in larger areas of preserved forest.

The river systems host a wide range of life from the common brook trout to the endangered freshwater mussel. Salamander and crayfish can be seen in streams by the quiet observer. Wild trout streams, stocked ponds and lakes, and seasonal Chesapeake Bay runs of rockfish and croaker provide variety for anglers.

The region's wildlife has witnessed many successes under the federal Endangered Species Act, perhaps none as stirring as the return of a viable bald eagle population. Places like Mason Neck Wildlife Refuge and other preserves along the lower Potomac are renowned nesting and viewing sites. How apropos that sightings of our national bird, virtually extinct thirty years ago, are becoming more and more common around our nation's capital.

WILDERNESS RESTRICTIONS/REGULATIONS

Public lands in the region fall into three broad categories: national parks and refuges; state parks, forests, and natural areas; private conservancy lands that are open to public use; and municipal parks.

Each entity has its own set of regulations. What's more, this book covers portions of three states and the District of Columbia, each with its own rules and operating procedures covering everything from pets to refuse (e.g., Maryland state parks are trash-free, requiring you to pack it out with you). But as you take advantage of this spectacular region, remember that our planet is very dear, very special, and very fragile. All of us should do everything we can to keep it clean, beautiful, and healthy, including following the Green Tips you'll find throughout this book.

You'll find varying degrees of public use among these designations. For example, hunting is allowed in some forests and parks, while wildlife refuges exist for the benefit of animals, not humans. Sections may be closed off to the public during breeding seasons. Conversely, federal, state, and municipal parks exist for humans, a fact reflected in their sometimes crowded conditions.

In the following chapters, we've strived to give you the most accurate, thorough, and up-to-date information on regulations and public use. When in doubt, we give you contact information so you can call ahead.

The author signs in to the trail register at Cedarville State Forest (Hike 4).

AREA CODES

The Washington, D.C., area code is 202. Northern Virginia area codes are 703, 571, and 540. Area codes for Maryland areas covered in this book are 301 and 240. The area code for all of West Virginia is 304.

ROADS

For current information on Washington, D.C., road conditions, weather, and closures, contact the District Department of Transportation at (202) 727-1000, or visit http://ddot.dc.gov, where you can sign up for automatic road updates by e-mail. For Virginia conditions contact the Virginia Department of Transportation (VDOT) twenty-four-hour Highway Helpline at (800) 367-7623 or visit www.vdot .state.va.us. For Maryland conditions contact the Maryland State Highway Administration at (410) 545-0300 or visit www.sha.state.md.us. For West Virginia's current road conditions, call (877) WVA-ROAD or visit www.wvdot.com.

Canada Geese in wetlands of Mason Neck State Park (Hike 21)

BY AIR

Dulles International Airport (IAD) is 23 miles northwest of downtown Washington, D.C. Ronald Reagan Washington National Airport (DCA) is located in Arlington, Virginia, just across the Potomac River from D.C. The Web site for both is www.mwaa.com. Baltimore/Washington International Thurgood Marshall Airport (BWI) is located between the two cities. The Web site is www.bwiairport.com.

To book reservations online, check out your favorite airline's Web site or search one of the following travel sites for the best price: www.cheaptickets.com, www.expedia.com, www.previewtravel.com, www.orbitz.com, www.priceline.com, http://travel.yahoo.com, www.travelocity.com, or www.trip.com—just to name a few.

BY RAIL

Washington, D.C., is served by AMTRAK. Schedules and pricing are at www.amtrak.com or by calling (800) 872-7245. Washington Metropolitan Area Transit Authority (known as "the Metro") operates rail and bus service throughout D.C. and suburbs in Maryland and Virginia. Visit www.wmata.com or call (202) 637-7000. Virginia Railway Express (VRE) operates commuter rail service weekdays to Fredericksburg and Manassas. For more information visit www.vre.org or call (800) RIDE-VRE. Maryland Rail Commuter (MARC) operates commuter rail service weekdays along the Potomac River in Maryland with an important stop for hikers in Harpers Ferry, West Virginia. For more information visit www.mtamaryland.com or call (800) 543-9809.

BY BUS

In addition to Metrobus (see By Rail), Greyhound serves many towns in the region; call (800) 231-2222 or visit www.greyhound.com for more information.

VISITOR INFORMATION

For general information on Virginia, visit the Web site of the Virginia Tourism Corporation, www.virginia.org, or call (800) 321-3244. For general information on Maryland, visit the Web site of the Maryland Office of Tourism, www.visitmaryland.org, or call (866) 639-3526. For information on visiting Washington, D.C., visit the Web site of Destination DC, www.washington.org, or call (800) 422-8644. For general information on West Virginia, visit the Web site of the West Virginia Division of Tourism, www.wvtourism.com, or call (800) 225-5982.

How to Use This Guide

Take a close enough look, and you'll find that this guide contains just about everything you'll ever need to choose, plan for, enjoy, and survive a hike near Washington, D.C. Stuffed with useful D.C.–area information, *Best Hikes Near Washington, D.C.* features thirty mapped and cued hikes. Here's an outline of the book's major components:

Each section begins with an **introduction to the region,** in which you're given a sweeping look at the lay of the land. Each hike then starts with a short **summary** of the hike's highlights. These quick overviews give you a taste of the hiking adventures to follow. You'll learn about the trail terrain and what surprises each route has to offer. Many chapters also include a **Kid Appeal** recommendation that provides parents with a quick reference for keeping their youngster engaged.

Following the overview you'll find the **hike specs:** quick, nitty-gritty details of the hike. Most are self-explanatory, but here are some details on others:

Distance: The total distance of the recommended route—one-way for loop hikes, the round-trip on an out-and-back or lollipop hike, point-to-point for a shuttle. Options are additional.

Approximate hiking time: The average time it will take to cover the route. It is based on the total distance, elevation gain, and condition and difficulty of the trail. Your fitness level will also affect your time.

Difficulty: Each hike has been assigned a level of difficulty. The rating system was developed from several sources and personal experience. These levels are meant to be a guideline only and may prove easier or harder for different people depending on ability and physical fitness.

Easy—Five miles or less total trip distance in one day, with minimal elevation gain, and paved or smooth-surfaced dirt trail.

Moderate—Up to 10 miles total trip distance in one day, with moderate elevation gain and potentially rough terrain.

Difficult—More than 10 miles total trip distance in one day, strenuous elevation gains, and rough and/or rocky terrain.

Trail surface: General information about what to expect underfoot.

Seasons: General information on the best time of year to hike.

Other trail users: Such as horseback riders, mountain bikers, inline skaters, etc.

Handicapped accessibility: When available we describe the features that make a park or a trail accessible to people with disabilities.

Canine compatibility: Know the trail regulations before you take your dog hiking with you. Dogs are not allowed on several trails in this book.

Land status: National forest, county open space, national park wilderness, etc.

Fees and permits: Whether you need to carry any money with you for park entrance fees and permits.

Schedule: Information on when the hike area is open.

Facilities: Amenities available at the trailhead or along the route.

Maps: This is a list of other maps to supplement the maps in this book. USGS maps are the best source for accurate topographical information, but the local park map may show more recent trails. Use both.

Trail contacts: This is the location, phone number, and Web site URL for the local land manager(s) in charge of all the trails within the selected hike. Before you head out, get trail access information, or contact the land manager after your visit if you see problems with trail erosion, damage, or misuse.

Other: Other information that will enhance your hike.

Special considerations: This section calls your attention to specific trail hazards, like a lack of water or hunting seasons.

The **Finding the trailhead** section gives you dependable driving directions to where you'll want to park. **The Hike** is the meat of the chapter. Detailed and honest, it's a carefully researched impression of the trail. It also often includes lots of area history, both natural and human. Under **Miles and Directions,** mileage cues identify all turns and trail name changes, as well as points of interest. **Options** are also given for many hikes to make your journey shorter or longer depending on the amount of

A hand-held GPS unit and a digital voice recorder are the authors' tools of the trade.

time you have. The **Hike Information** section provides information on local events and attractions, restaurants, hiking tours, and hiking organizations.

Don't feel restricted to the routes and trails that are mapped here. Be adventurous and use this guide as a platform to discover new routes for yourself. One of the simplest ways to begin this is to just turn the map upside down and hike any route in reverse. The change in perspective is often fantastic, and the hike should feel quite different. With this in mind, it'll be like getting two distinctly different hikes on each map. For your own purposes, you may wish to copy the route directions onto a small sheet of paper to help you while hiking, or photocopy the map and cue sheet to take with you. Otherwise, just slip the whole book in your backpack and take it all with you. Enjoy your time in the outdoors and remember to pack out what you pack in.

HOW TO USE THE MAPS

Overview map: This map shows the location of each hike in the area by hike number.

Route map: This is your primary guide to each hike. It shows all of the accessible roads and trails, points of interest, water, landmarks, and geographical features. It also distinguishes trails from roads, and paved roads from unpaved roads. The selected route is highlighted, and directional arrows point the way.

A wild turkey

Map Legend

Transportation

🛡 95 Freeway/Interstate Highway

🛡 1 U.S. Highway

🛡 4 State Highway

1431 Other Road

Unpaved Road

Railroad

Trails

Selected Route

Trail or Fire Road

→ Direction of Travel

Water Features

Body of Water

River or Creek

Marsh

Waterfalls

Land Management

Local & State Parks

National Forest &
Wilderness Areas

Symbols

✈ Airport

⤫ Bridge

■ Building/Point of Interest

▲ Campground

⦙ Gate

♿ Handicap Parking Area

▲ Mountain/Peak

🗼 Observation Platform

🅿 Parking

🅰 Picnic Area

👥 Ranger Station

🚻 Restroom

📷 Scenic View

⫼ Steps

○ Towns and Cities

20 Trailhead

❓ Visitor Center

Trail Finder

Hike No.	Hike Name	Best Hikes for Beach/Coast Lovers	Best Hikes for History Lovers	Best Hikes for Waterfalls	Best Hikes for Geology/Fossils	Best Hikes for Children	Best Hikes for Dogs	Best Hikes for Great Views	Best Hikes for Bird Lovers	Best Hikes for Tree Huggers	Best Hikes for Handicapped Accessibility
1	American Chestnut Land Trust						•				
2	Calvert Cliffs State Park	•			•	•				•	
3	Catoctin Mountain Park		•			•	•	•			
4	Cedarville State Forest					•	•				
5	Cunningham Falls State Park			•		•	•	•			•
6	Gambrill State Park					•	•				
7	Great Falls Park, MD/Chesapeake and Ohio Canal National Historic Park		•	•	•	•		•			•
8	Jug Bay Natural Area (Patuxent River Park) Loops	•				•	•		•		
9	Patuxent National Wildlife Refuge						•		•		•
10	Rosaryville State Park						•		•	•	
11	Seneca Creek Greenway Trail North (#1)				•	•	•			•	
12	Seneca Creek Greenway Trail South (#2)		•		•	•	•				
13	Sugarloaf Mountain		•		•	•	•	•			
14	Arlington National Cemetery		•								•

Trail Finder

Hike No.	Hike Name	Best Hikes for Beach/Coast Lovers	Best Hikes for History Lovers	Best Hikes for Waterfalls	Best Hikes for Geology/Fossils	Best Hikes for Children	Best Hikes for Dogs	Best Hikes for Great Views	Best Hikes for Bird Lovers	Best Hikes for Tree Huggers	Best Hikes for Handicapped Accessibility
15	Bull Run Mountains Conservancy		●		●	●		●		●	
16	Great Falls Park			●		●	●	●			●
17	G. Richard Thompson Wildlife Management Area					●				●	
18	Harpers Ferry, VA/MD/WV		●			●	●	●			●
19	Leesylvania State Park	●	●			●	●				●
20	Manassas National Battlefield Park		●				●				●
21	Mason Neck State Park		●			●	●		●		●
22	Overall Run, SNP			●			●	●			
23	Piney River, SNP		●	●		●	●			●	
24	Prince William Forest Park				●	●	●			●	●
25	Riverbend Park					●	●		●		●
26	Sky Meadows State Park		●			●	●	●			
27	Wildcat Mountain Natural Area		●							●	
28	Georgetown Loop (Rock Creek Park South)		●			●	●				●
29	National Mall Monuments		●			●					●
30	Rock Creek Park North		●			●	●		●		●

By and large, these habits and manners have all but faded in the day-to-day bustle and spread of suburbia. To all, that is, except the hiker. It is our happy lot to find the remains of old mills along the stream valley parks, like Black Rock Mill on the Great Seneca Creek. We can appreciate the backbreaking labor to build a charcoal pit or walk through the dark swamps that hid presidential assassin John Wilkes Booth in 1865.

We've walked only 100 miles or so from the water's edge to the mountains. A small region packed with so much to see.

Trailhead in Rosaryville State Park (Hike 10)

American Chestnut Land Trust

Parkers Creek is the centerpiece of the American Chestnut Land Trust's 810-acre holdings in Calvert County. The creek's tidal salt marshes, upland forest of oak and hickory, and its many tributaries are billed as the last undeveloped watershed on the Chesapeake Bay's western shore. Of the described routes here, only those departing from Double Oak Farm (north tract) offer hikers glimpses of the stream. The south tract, covering old family farms, cemeteries, and a burgeoning beaver community, has its own special character as you explore muddy footpaths along Gravatt Stream and Jett Stream.

NORTH TRACT

Start: From the American Chestnut Land Trust's Double Oak Farm trailhead
Distance: Option 1: Horse Swamp Trail, 3.0-mile out-and-back; Option 2: Parkers Creek Loop, 4.1 miles
Approximate hiking time: 2 hours
Difficulty: Easy due to well-marked paths and only moderate elevation loss and gain. Of either hike, Horse Swamp Trail features terrain that is steeper—but even these are of short duration.
Trail surface: Both routes begin as mowed field paths but quickly adopt the character of the woodland that surrounds their namesake streams. Upland trails are old farm roads, while stream valley paths are single-track dirt paths that span low elevation and wetland via footbridges and boardwalks.

SOUTH TRACT

Start: From the American Chestnut Land Trust's Scientists Cliffs Road trailhead
Distance: Option 3: 4.7-mile loop
Approximate hiking time: 2 to 3 hours
Difficulty: Easy due to the short distance, minimum elevation gain, and wide, easy-to-follow paths
Trail surface: Old dirt farm roads characterize the upland paths. In the stream valleys, along Gravatt Stream and the Jett Stream, narrow footpaths have more woodsy and scenic character.
Seasons: Best in spring or autumn, seasons that coincide with the height of bird and beaver activity
Other trail users: Horseback riders, joggers, cross-country skiers
Canine compatibility: Leashed dogs permitted
Land status: Private land trust
Fees and permits: No fees

required. Groups of more than 10 people are encouraged to apply for a group permit.

Schedule: Open dawn to dusk, 365 days a year. Turkey hunting in springtime will affect hikers who seek to visit from dawn to 12:30 p.m. on certain days in Apr and May. Contact the land trust for specific dates.

Facilities: Picnic tables and a chemical toilet at the north trailhead

Maps: DeLorme *Maryland/Delaware Atlas & Gazetteer:* Page 38 D3. USGS 7.5 minute series: *Prince Frederick, MD.* Trail maps are free and available at trail registers.

Trail contacts: American Chestnut Land Trust, Double Oak Road, Prince Frederick, MD 20678; (410) 414-3400; www.acltweb.org

Special considerations: The land trust requests that all visitors sign in at trail registers located at both parking areas. Groups are limited to 10 people or fewer. The land trust holds a special Deer Harvest Program each fall.

Finding the trailhead:

Distance from Washington, D.C.: 49 miles

Double Oak Farm from the junction of MD 4 and MD 2 in Sunderland: Drive south on combined MD 2/4 (Solomons Island Road) for 8 miles. In Prince Frederick, turn left (east) on MD 402 (Dares Beach Road). In 2.3 miles, turn right (south) onto Double Oak Road. Follow this road for another 3.2 miles, and then veer left onto a gravel road. There is a metal gate (open during park hours) and signs for American Chestnut Land Trust property. It is 0.3 mile to Double Oak Farm. Enter a gravel parking area adjacent to an equipment shed. Access to both Horse Swamp and the Parkers Creek Loop begins at a trailboard sign next to the equipment shed. Trailhead GPS: N38 32.821' / W76 31.982'

Scientists Cliffs from Prince Frederick: Continue south on MD 2/4 through Prince Frederick. Approaching the town of Port Republic, look for brown signs indicating the American Chestnut Land Trust. In 5 miles from Prince Frederick, turn left (east) on Parkers Creek Road. Immediately cross over MD 765 (Old Solomons Island Road). Go 0.4 mile and turn right (south) on Scientists Cliffs Road. In another 0.8 mile, turn left (east) into the American Chestnut Land Trust parking lot. There is an equipment shed with a porch near the field. Gravatt Lane/Swamp Trail begins at a cable across a farm road near the entrance to the parking lot. Trailhead GPS: N38 30.752' / W76 31.112'

THE HIKE

The American Chestnut Land Trust (ACLT) is named for a tree. It succumbed to the chestnut blight, a disease introduced to the United States in 1900. Within forty years, the blight had traveled down the Appalachian chain, destroying a climax forest that had stood for thousands of years. In mountain areas, American chestnut trees are often the standing white trunks, bare of any bark, ghostly white, like tree skeletons amid an otherwise healthy forest.

A note at the southern tract trailhead for the ACLT states simply: Losing this tree is a sad reminder that all things in Nature must be enjoyed and protected while they are here.

The same could be said for land that is owned or managed by the land trust. Upland farms on both sides of Parkers Creek protect what the trust describes as the "only pristine marsh on the western shore of the Chesapeake Bay." Although in its history this area has seen tobacco farms and related settlements, it is absent these activities today. Old fields are now thick forests of Virginia pine or the succession hardwood forest of maples, oaks, hickories, and black walnuts.

Choosing which tract to explore—the northern trails leave from Double Oak Farms, headquarters for the land trust; southern trails leave from an unattended trailhead on Scientists Cliff Road—is a choice between experiencing Parkers Creek firsthand or exploring a dynamic farms-to-woodland habitat. Both the Horse Swamp Trail and the Parkers Creek Loop, accessed via the northern tract, are easy routes that descend to overlooks over the stream. In the fall, the marsh grass is golden brown. Come springtime, it shows a fresh green tint. At the junction of Old Parkers Creek Road, where a bridge once spanned the creek, it is possible to sit, in the closing hours of the day, and wait for the loud slap sound of a beaver tail. The forest floor bursts with mayapple in spring and large specimens of jack-in-the-pulpit. The handful of small tributaries crossed on Parkers Creek Trail show the broad leaves of three typical freshwater marshes: arrow arum, spatterdock, and pickerelweed. The last shows characteristic purple flowers in spring. All three plants are valuable food sources for wood ducks and other waterfowl, including migratory shorebirds like the sorrel and black rail.

From the southern tract trailhead on Scientists Cliff Road, Gravatt Lane offers the quickest access to what's interesting. Splitting from it onto Swamp Trail, you descend to follow a small tributary. At the cutoff for the chestnut tree memorial, a sign warns that ahead, a boardwalk over a large marsh is closed due to heavy beaver activity. Continue walking—a visit to the marsh, while it means backtracking, is still a valuable experience. By late spring, the mayapple leaves have taken on a yellowish hue, adding a new color to the brown- and tan-tinged understory thick with fallen leaves.

The marsh boardwalk extends out for several hundred feet over ground that is knee-high in water in spring but considerably less wet come late summer and

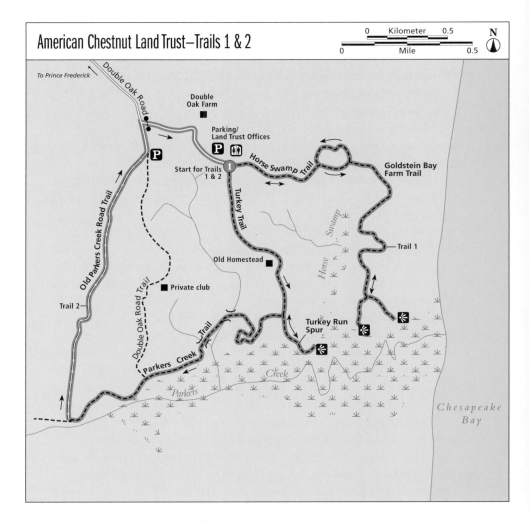

fall. A morning chorus of bullfrogs—a descending, bowlike note—and songbirds keep up at a steady pace. Scarlet tanagers, red-eyed vireos, and wood thrushes are present. The wood thrush is especially present as evening falls, its multipitched, multisyllable call filtering down from the darkening woods.

MILES AND DIRECTIONS

Trail 1: Horse Swamp

0.0   START from a trailboard map at the Double Oak Farm trailhead parking lot. Follow Horse Swamp Trail, a mowed path, through a field, passing the trailhead for Turkey Trail en route. At the far side of the field, follow the yellow-blazed trail into the woods and descend on a wide dirt path. (**Note:** Turkey Trail is the first leg of the Parkers Creek Loop.)

0.5 Veer right at a junction with the return leg of Horse Swamp Trail.

0.6 Stay straight, cross Horse Swamp on a footbridge, and merge onto the red-blazed Goldstein Bay Farm Trail.

1.5 Reach a fork in the trail. Both spurs, to the right and left, lead to overlooks of Parkers Creek. (**FYI:** Views from both overlooks are limited in summertime due to the trees and leaves blocking them.)

1.7 After exploring both spurs and overlooks, hike north on Goldstein Bay Farm Trail.

2.4 Cross Horse Swamp on a footbridge and turn right (north) to merge onto Horse Swamp Trail. Cross a 30-foot-long boardwalk, and then start climbing the hillside.

2.5 Turn right onto the northern leg of the loop.

2.6 Bear right (south) as the Horse Swamp Trail finishes its loop.

3.0 HIKE ENDS at the Double Oak Farm trailhead parking lot.

Trail 2: Parkers Creek

0.0 START from the junction of Horse Swamp Trail and Turkey Trail, 60 feet east of the Double Oak Farm trailhead parking lot. Turn right (south) on Turkey Trail. (**FYI:** A number of signs alongside this trail help interpret the natural surroundings and the historic Scales/Simmons home site.)

0.5 The trail levels briefly at the site of an old homestead, then continues its descent to Parkers Creek.

0.6 Stay straight (south) at the junction with Parkers Creek Trail and merge onto Turkey Run Spur, an out-and-back trail that descends to the marshy fringes of Parkers Creek.

0.9 Spur trail ends. Turn around and return to Parkers Creek Trail.

1.2 Turn left (west) onto Parkers Creek Trail.

1.6 Descend into a gully and cross a tributary of Parkers Creek. Ahead, another footbridge and corduroys (hewn logs laid side by side) help you navigate over low, wet sections of trail.

2.2 Stay straight (west) on Parkers Creek Trail at a junction with Double Oak Road Trail on the right.

2.4 Turn right (north) onto Old Parkers Creek Road Trail. (**Side trip:** Detour left to the water's edge, where a bridge once spanned the creek. This area is high with beaver activity.)

3.7 Emerge from woods onto Double Oak Road. Turn left (north) and walk up the paved road.

3.8 Turn right onto the gravel driveway that leads to the Double Oak Farm headquarters.

4.1 HIKE ENDS at the Double Oak Farm trailhead parking lot.

Trail 3: South Trails

0.0 START from the Scientists Cliffs Road trailhead, at the south end of the parking area. Gravatt Lane/Swamp Trail is blocked to traffic by a cable. Follow Gravatt Lane straight (north) down a tree-shaded farm road that divides fields on your left and right. (**Note:** Avoid trailheads for Bloodroot and Flint Trails, which veer left [west] and cross the field to the woodland beyond.)

0.2 Turn right (east) and pass a wooden outhouse on your right. (**Note:** Wallace Lane continues straight to a junction with Bloodroot Trail in 0.1 miles.)

0.3 Veer right (east) on Swamp Trail at a fork.

0.7 Stay straight (north) on Swamp Trail at a junction with the Chestnut Trail on the left. (**FYI:** Signs here indicate the trail ahead is closed at the Beaver Dam.)

1.0 Stay straight (north) on Swamp Trail past an unmarked trail that branches left.

1.05 Stay straight (north) on Swamp Trail as an unmarked trail branches right. (**Note:** This is the access trail to Cemetery Lane.)

1.1 Reach the end of the boardwalk, turn around, and return to the Cemetery Lane access trail.

1.15 Turn left on the Cemetery Lane access trail and climb to the top of a small ridge.

1.2 Turn right on Cemetery Lane.

1.5 Reach the Hance-Chesley Cemetery. Explore, then retrace your steps to the Swamp Trail.

1.8 Turn left (south) on the Swamp Trail.

ACLT's southern tract harbored Maryland's largest American chestnut tree. The specimen finally succumbed to the blight that has virtually wiped out the tree from East Coast forests, although its ancient, decayed trunk and root system still sends up young shoots. GPS: N38 30.969' / W76 31.139'

Remains of an ancient American Chestnut

2.3 Turn right (west) on the Chestnut Trail. The landmark chestnut tree is marked on the left side of the trail as you climb. (It succumbed to the chestnut blight that affects all American chestnut trees; suckers, or shoots, now stem from the rotted trunk.)

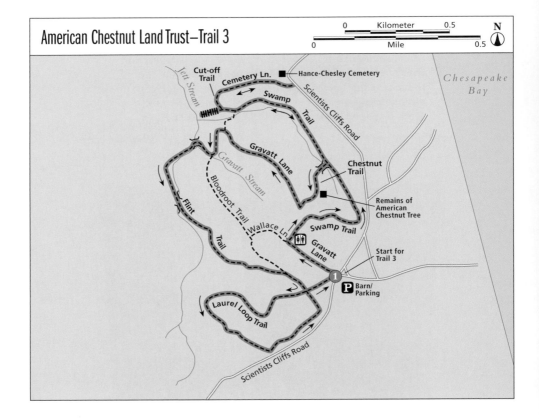

Kilometer
0   0.5
Mile
0   0.5
N

2.4   Turn right (north) on Gravatt Lane.

2.9   Cross Gravatt Stream on a footbridge, then turn right (north) on the yellow-blazed Flint Trail. Ahead, the trail crosses small streams three times on footbridges.

3.3   Bear right on Flint Trail to cross a boardwalk over a wetland. Avoid an unmarked, less-defined trail that forks left and climbs the hillside.

3.6   Turn right (south) on Bloodroot Trail.

3.7   Reach a Y junction and turn right (west) on Laurel Loop Trail.

4.0   Cross a stream on a footbridge and begin climbing the hillside opposite.

4.6   Turn right (east) on Bloodroot Trail. Descend to a field and cross diagonally right, heading toward the road.

4.7   HIKE ENDS at the Gravatt Lane/Swamp Trail trailhead.

HIKE INFORMATION

Local information: Calvert County Chamber of Commerce, Prince Frederick, MD; (410) 535-2577; www.calvertchamber.org

Chesapeake Bay Gateways Network, Annapolis, MD; (800) YOUR BAY (800-968-7229); www.baygateways.net. This is an initiative of the National Park Service Chesapeake Bay Program Office, including more than 150 parks, wildlife refuges, museums, and hiking, biking, paddling, and driving trails that promote the Chesapeake Bay's natural and cultural history.

Local events/attractions: December: Greens Sale and Beach Hayride

Good eats: Robert's Fresh Baked Deli, 135 Dares Beach Rd., Prince Frederick, MD; (410) 535-3944. Great sandwiches and homemade pretzels in an out-of-the-way cafe bar.

Hike tours: Volunteers and staff members lead guided nature hikes and canoe trips seasonally.

Hance-Chesley Cemetery

Calvert Cliffs State Park

A shallow sea once covered all of southern Maryland. When it receded twenty to twenty-five million years ago, the steep shoreline now known as Calvert Cliffs were exposed and began to erode. They're still eroding today (making them dangerous to walk on), continually revealing the East Coast's largest assemblage of fossils—over 600 species of sharks, whales, rays, and seabirds that were the size of small airplanes!

Start: From the Red Trail parking area at the edge of a small pond

Distance: 4.6-mile loop

Approximate hiking time: 3 hours

Difficulty: Easy due to a minimum of elevation gain; well-marked, graded trails; and easy terrain

Trail surface: A combination of boardwalk and sandy roads mark the main stem of the trail network. Dirt footpaths alternate between low streamside terrain and upland forests.

Seasons: Jun through Sept, when a hot hike out to the bay is relieved with a little bit of wading along the shoreline

Other trail users: Bikers, hunters, cross-country skiers, runners

Canine compatibility: Dogs not permitted

Land status: State park

Fees and permits: Per-vehicle entrance fee

Schedule: Sunrise to sunset daily

Facilities: Restrooms, picnic area, playground

Maps: DeLorme *Maryland/Delaware Atlas & Gazetteer:* Page 31 B4. USGS: *Cove Point, MD. Calvert Cliffs State Park Trail Guide,* a waterproof topographic map, is available online at http://dnr.maryland.gov/publiclands/trailguides.html or by mail from the Maryland Department of Natural Resources, Maryland Park Service, Attn: Trail Guides, 580 Taylor Ave., E-3, Annapolis, MD 21401.

Trail contacts: Calvert Cliffs State Park, c/o Smallwood State Park, 2750 Sweden Point Rd., Marbury, MD 20658; physical location of Calvert Cliffs: 9500 H. G. Truman Parkway, Lusby, MD, (301) 743-7613; www.dnr.state.md.us/publiclands/southern/calvertcliffs.html

Finding the trailhead:

Distance from Washington, D.C.: 56 miles

From Prince Frederick: Drive south on MD 2/4. Four miles south of Port Republic, turn left on MD 765/Solomons Island Road. Pass through the small hamlet of Lusby and drive south another mile to the park entrance. Turn left (east) on the park entrance road and follow the one-way road to the pay station. Continue past a maintenance shed and bathroom on the right, and descend to a parking area at the edge of a pond. Trailhead GPS: N38 23.695' / W76 26.091'

THE HIKE

In the annals of great North American explorations, many are familiar with the exploits of Lewis and Clark, who explored land from the Mississippi to the Pacific from 1804 to 1806. But nearly 200 years earlier, Capt. John Smith led a crew of fourteen men out into the Chesapeake Bay in the summer of 1608. Using a small boat powered by sail and oars, they left Jamestown Settlement and sailed into the Chesapeake Bay. Their journey touched on the eastern shore of Virginia and Maryland, and the western shore from the top of the Bay to Hampton Roads in the south. The reaches of great rivers like the Patuxent, Potomac, Rappahannock, and other smaller streams were explored as far as the flat water would allow.

Calvert beach

Smith's goals were derived from a charter from the London Company, which financed the Jamestown project. One was to locate a "northwest passage" to India. Another was to explore and document as much land, creeks, and bays as possible, and to claim those lands for the English crown. As a result, Smith compiled most of the information known about Native Americans and the ecology of the Chesapeake Bay region in the 1600s.

So it is with Calvert Cliffs. After exploring the Nanticoke River, Smith abandoned further exploration of the Eastern Shore and struck west to cross the Bay. He used as a landmark a set of tall cliffs that were lit up by the morning sun on the day of the crossing.

"Finding this eastern shore shallow broken isles, and for the most part without fresh water, we passed by the straits of Limbo for the western shore. So broad is the Bay here we could scarce perceive the great high cliffs on the other side. By them we anchored that night and called them Rickard's Cliffs." (Capt. John Smith's journal)

Smith named locations for local Native American tribes but also for men on his voyage. So it is that what is known today as Tangier Island was originally named Russell Isles for the doctor who accompanied them. The source of Rickard's Cliffs is thought to be Smith's mother (who was not on the trip), who came from "Rickards, at the Great Heck, in Yorkshire" (England).

The cliffs that line the Maryland shore are a geologic phenomenon. They were formed between six and twenty million years ago and contain some of the largest Miocene fossil deposits in the world. The Red Trail is the "superhighway" for fossil seekers at Calvert Cliffs State Park. Access to the cliff line of these 130-foot-high banks is blocked because of erosion problems; walking the base of the cliff line is prohibited as well due to landslides.

As a geologic feature, the cliffs that can be glimpsed at the mouth of Grays Creek in Calvert Cliffs State Park are one piece of a line that continues north to Chesapeake Beach. They are justly famous. According to the Maryland Geological Survey, the first fossil described from North America was found in deposits of the St. Mary's Formation, which constitutes the youngest geologic formation present at Calvert Cliffs. That record was published in an English journal in 1865, some 257 years after John Smith had used the cliffs as a beacon to help his corps of explorers cross the Chesapeake Bay.

MILES AND DIRECTIONS

0.0 START from a parking lot and trail signboard at the edge of a pond. Locate the Red Trail trailhead and follow this dirt and crushed-rock path to a boardwalk along the pond's south shoreline. A sign at this trailhead points toward the Cliff Trail and the parking area.

0.1 Veer right and avoid a footpath that leads uphill to the left.

0.2 Turn right where the Red Trail, until now a sandy footpath, merges with a gravel-lined forest road.

0.3 Turn right off the gravel road and follow the Red Trail, which is now a dirt footpath.

0.35 Stay straight as the Yellow Trail intersects with the Red Trail on the right. (**Note:** This junction marks the return portion of this route.)

0.6 Stay straight as a dirt road merges with the Red Trail on the left.

0.7 Stay straight as the Blue Trail merges with the Red Trail from the right. The trail here is hard-packed sand, and the footing is uneven over exposed tree roots.

1.4 Pass a boardwalk that leads to a viewing platform on Grays Creek.

1.6 At a junction with a gravel service road, turn right (east).

1.8 The Red Trail ends at the Chesapeake Bay. After exploring the beach at the mouth of Grays Creek, begin to retrace your steps on the Red Trail. (**FYI:** The high cliffs to the left [north] are closed to the public due to erosion and landslides.)

2.0 Stay right on the gravel road as the Red Trail branches left (west) as a footpath.

2.1 After a brief climb, the service road levels at a left bend. Turn right here onto the Orange Trail, a wide dirt footpath.

2.3 Cross Thomas Branch on a boardwalk.

2.8 At a fork in the Orange Trail, bear left onto an unmarked footpath that descends through the woods. Within 0.1 mile, merge onto the White Trail, which enters from the right.

3.2 Turn left (east) onto a gravel service road. Walk 50 feet and turn right (south) onto a wide footpath that leads downhill. An arrow at this trail junction reads ACCESS TO RED TRAIL.

3.3 Turn right (west) onto the Red Trail.

3.4 Veer left (south) onto the Blue Trail. Immediately cross Grays Creek on a footbridge. The trail is a sandy footpath, and mileage markers are in descending order as you head south through the woods.

4.0 Turn right (north) onto the Yellow Trail. The trail begins to descend along a seasonal tributary of Grays Creek.

Calvert Cliffs State Park

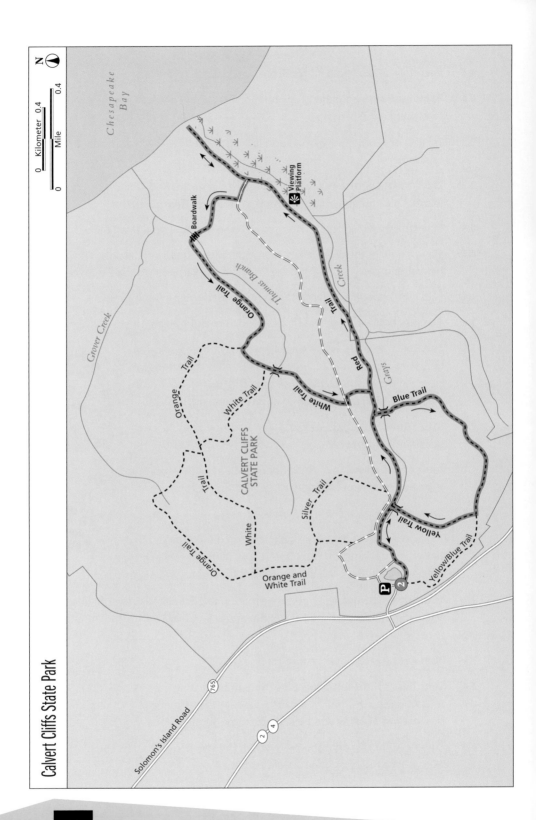

N

0 Kilometer 0.4
0 Mile 0.4

Chesapeake Bay

Grover Creek

CALVERT CLIFFS STATE PARK

Orange Trail

White Trail

Orange Trail

White Trail

White Trail

Silver Trail

Orange and White Trail

Boardwalk

Orange Trail

Thomas Branch

Viewing Platform

Red Trail

Grays Creek

Blue Trail

Yellow Trail

Yellow/Blue Trail

P

2

Solomon's Island Road

765

2

4

4.3 Turn left (west) on the Red Trail.

4.6 HIKE ENDS at the trailboard and parking area at the edge of a pond.

HIKE INFORMATION

Local information: Calvert County Department of Economic Development, Courthouse, Prince Frederick, MD; (800) 331-9771; www.ecalvert.com
Solomons Information Center, 14175 Solomons Island Rd. S., Solomons, MD; (410) 326-6027

Local events/attractions: Calvert Marine Museum, State Route 2, Solomons, MD; (410) 326-2042; www.calvertmarinemuseum.com. Premiere museum about life on the Chesapeake Bay.

Good eats: The Frying Pan, 9825 H G Truman Rd., Lusby, MD; (410) 326-1125. On the way to the park, a casual mom-and-pop place for a big, inexpensive breakfast.

Organizations: Friends of Calvert Cliffs State Park, Lusby, MD; (410) 394-1778

It's all about the shark's tooth. A short stretch of Bay shoreline is open to the public, and it attracts kids of all ages searching for the elusive prehistoric prize: a shark's tooth. Stick to the Red Trail for the most direct route to and from the water. Best collecting is usually after a storm, when the supply of shells and other fossils is replenished. Low tide, when more beach is exposed, is the best time to look for fossils.

Boardwalk over bog

A hiker following this route will pass a threshold (unmarked, undeclared, and usually unnoticed), like the Continental Divide, that signals a shift in the underlying bedrock. The trail from Wolf Rock descends almost to Park Central Road, and thereafter it climbs to Blue Ridge Summit Overlook. Undetected is a change in the underlying bedrock, from the white quartzite of Chimney Rock and Wolf Rock to the Catoctin greenstone. It is from this park that the stone received its name, and it's fitting as you look off Hog Rock, on the second leg of this route, that the stone beneath your feet is, in name and spirit, one and the same.

Catoctin was only 100 miles from the edge of the ice sheet and, as such, had a climate that is described as near glacial: permafrost, tundra, and fluctuations of freezing and thawing temperatures. Ideal conditions, in other words, for rocks like the sturdy quartzite, which makes up the citadel-like fortress known as Chimney Rock, to break up along fault lines. These broken-up bits then

---

KID APPEAL

Interpretive signs on the 0.5-mile Charcoal Trail tell the story of charcoal making in the 1800s. Hundreds of woodcutters were employed to produce the charcoal, which in turn fueled the Catoctin Iron Furnace. The trail starts at the Thurmont Vista parking lot on Park Central Road.

Chimney Rock, Catoctin Mountain Park Courtesy of the Tourism Council of Frederick County, MD

Hog Rock Nature Trail

As you reenter the woods opposite the Hog Rock parking area, look for a box nailed to a tree that holds a printed interpretive pamphlet. It describes the typical species, each assigned a number, that have repopulated the hills of Catoctin Mountain Park in the one hundred years since it was denuded of timber for the charcoal industry. A short 0.4-mile loop at Hog Rock Overlook has numbered posts that correspond with the sheet.

begin a slow migration downslope. A gradually warming climate, the retreat of the glaciers, and a stabilizing of temperatures brought an end to the conditions that facilitated the rock streams "slipping" down the slope. And so, as you scramble the rocks, the lichen and moss, as well as the small understory elms and beeches growing amid it, indicate a stabilization. A rock stream, frozen in time.

Catoctin Mountain Park has more recent stories to tell as well, and an excellent series of interpretive trails brings the park's past to life. As you descend from Wolf Rock to a four-way junction, consider a side trip to the Charcoal Trail, a 0.5-mile loop that describes how an industry built on timber denuded the hillsides of nearly every living tree.

MILES AND DIRECTIONS

0.0 START at a parking lot on MD 77 near two tall stone pillars that mark the driveway entrance to the national park's headquarters. Walk 250 feet west along the highway shoulder (with traffic) to a wood trail sign for Chimney Rock, Wolf Rock, and the visitor center. Enter the woods on a dirt woodland path and begin climbing.

0.3 Pass the lower trailhead for Crows Nest Loop on the right as the trail begins a series of switchbacks and crosses a stone stream indicated by the sheet of loose rock that covers the uphill slope.

0.6 Bear left (north) and uphill at a junction with the upper trailhead for Crows Nest Loop.

The presidential retreat, Camp David, is within the park. Portions of the television series **The West Wing** *were filmed here. The retreat is closed to the public and cannot be seen from any roads, but there is a Camp David Museum in the historic Cozy Restaurant in Thurmont.*

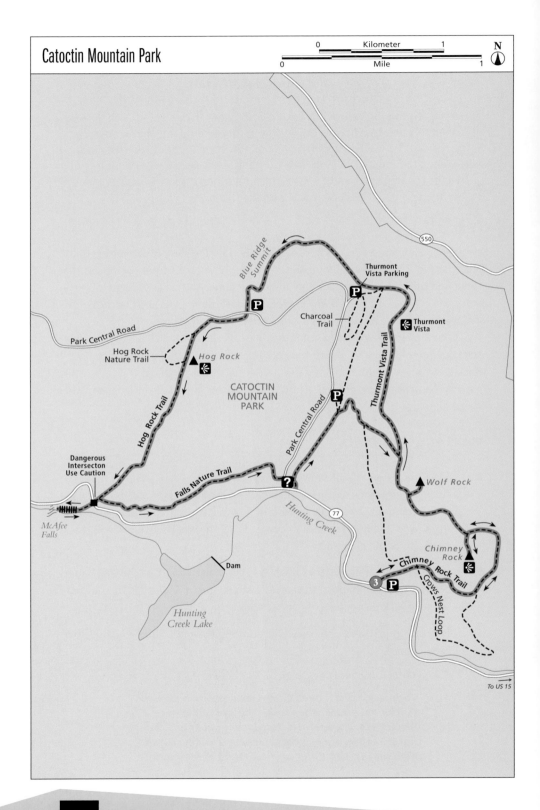

Catoctin Mountain Park

0 Kilometer 1
0 Mile 1

N

550

Blue Ridge Summit

Park Central Road

Hog Rock Nature Trail

Hog Rock

Thurmont Vista Parking

Charcoal Trail

Thurmont Vista

CATOCTIN MOUNTAIN PARK

Thurmont Vista Trail

Hog Rock Trail

Dangerous Intersecton Use Caution

Falls Nature Trail

Park Central Road

Wolf Rock

McAfee Falls

?

Hunting Creek

77

Chimney Rock

Dam

Chimney Rock Trail

3

Crows Nest Loop

Hunting Creek Lake

To US 15

1.0 Circle around house-size rock formations as the trail rises to a spur trail on the left leading to the citadel-like tower of Weaverton quartzite that make up Chimney Rock. Turn left on the spur trail to reach the rock formation.

1.5 A spur trail branches right to Wolf Rock. (**FYI:** Views from this rock outcrop are blocked by the trees, but it remains a popular spot as it is the only area in the park where rock climbing is permitted.)

2.5 Continue northward. Turn right on a short spur trail to a rest area at Thurmont Vista. Views are eastward to the small town of Thurmont and the wider Frederick Valley.

2.9 Turn right at a four-way intersection, following signs for Hog Rock. (**Bailout:** Turn left [south] and hike 0.5 mile to a four-way trail junction. Here, turn left, hike uphill, and return to the trailhead via Wolf Rock and Chimney Rock.)

3.6 After a short, steep climb, the trail levels atop Blue Ridge Summit. (**FYI:** In summertime, views northward are limited from rocks that parallel the trail for the next 0.1 mile, but the summit is nonetheless a fascinating spot to investigate the hardy ferns, mosses, and chestnut oaks that grow on these rocks.)

3.9 Walk straight through the Hog Rock parking lot, cross Park Central Road, and reenter woods on a dirt woods path.

4.2 Reach Hog Rock Overlook on the left. This exposed quartzite rock formation has all-season views eastward and is shaded by an unusually tall shagbark hickory tree. (**Option:** From this overlook continue straight on Hog Rock Trail, or turn right [west] onto Hog Rock Nature Trail, an interpretive trail that rejoins Hog Rock Trail in 0.4 mile.) Continue south on Hog Rock Trail.

5.2 Turn left (east) on Falls Nature Trail. (**Side trip:** Continue straight on Hog Rock Trail to where it ends at MD 77. Turn left and walk 50 paces east on the road shoulder, against traffic. Cross to the south side of the highway and enter a parking lot for McAfee Falls [also known as Cunningham Falls], which is reserved for handicapped visitors. Inside the parking area, follow a boardwalk leading 0.3 mile to the falls area.) (**Caution:** This MD 77 crossing occurs at a blind corner for vehicles traveling in both directions.)

The first youth Job Corps Center was established here in 1965 as part of President Lyndon Johnson's War on Poverty.

6.2 Enter the national park visitor center's west parking lot. Turn left and walk through the parking area, across Park Central Road into the east parking lot, and head for the far left corner. Climb a short flight of stone steps and enter the woods on the Thurmont Vista Trail.

6.8 Turn right (east) and hike uphill.

7.3 Merge right onto Chimney Rock Trail.

8.9 HIKE ENDS at the Chimney Rock trailhead.

HIKE INFORMATION

Local information: Tourism Council of Frederick County, 19 E. Church St., Frederick, MD; (301) 644-4047; www.fredericktourism.org

Local events/attractions: The Covered Bridge Driving Tour, www.frederick tourism.org/driving_coveredbridges.html. Passes three historic bridges on Old Frederick Road.

Good eats: The Cozy Restaurant, 103 Frederick Rd., Thurmont, MD; (301) 271-7373; www.cozyvillage.com. Oldest restaurant in Maryland, with a Camp David Museum inside.

Local outdoor stores: The Trail House, 17 S. Market St., Frederick, MD; (301) 694-8448; www.trailhouse.com. Has hiking supplies and maps.

Hike tours: TeamLink Mountain, Frederick, MD; (301) 695-1814; www.teamlink inc.com

An autumn trail in Catoctin Mountain Park Courtesy of the Tourism Council of Frederick County, MD

Cedarville State Forest

Cedarville State Forest protects Zekiah Swamp Run, ranked Maryland's most eco-logical diverse stream, notable for its rare and endangered plants. From its source in a moist bog of sphagnum moss, the stream moves sluggishly under a canopy of maples, sweetgum, and river birch. At its source grows the carnivorous roundleaf sundew and the northern pitcher plant.

Start: From a parking lot at the state forest visitor center

Distance: 13-mile loop

Approximate hiking time: 5 hours

Difficulty: Difficult due to length; terrain is easy

Trail surface: Dirt footpaths and old forest roads traverse a heavily wooded area, with short stretches through the watershed of two major streams. Low areas adjacent to streams may be flooded in peri-ods of heavy rain.

Seasons: Apr through Aug

Other trail users: Mountain bik-ers, horseback riders, hunters

Handicapped accessibility: Dis-abled hunting access and archery range

Canine compatibility: Dogs permitted

Land status: State forest

Fees and permits: Per-vehicle entrance fee

Schedule: Daily dawn to dusk

Facilities: Restrooms, visitor cen-ter, campground, playground, picnic pavilions, archery range, fish hatchery visitor center

Maps: DeLorme *Maryland/Dela-ware Atlas & Gazetteer:* Page 37 C6. USGS 7.5 minute series: *Bran-dywine, MD.* Custom topographic maps are sold at the state forest's visitor center, or online at http://dnr.maryland.gov/publiclands/trailguides.html. See also National Geographic's TOPO! software, Mid-Atlantic Region, Disc 4.

Trail contacts: Cedarville State Forest, 10201 Bee Oak Rd., Brandy-wine, MD 20613; (800) 784-5380; www.dnr.state.md.us/publiclands/cedarvilleguide.html

Special considerations: Be aware of hunting seasons, competitive archery ranges on the Blue Trail, trail washouts after heavy rains, and sharing the trail with moun-tain bikers, the Orange Trail in par-ticular.

Finding the trailhead:

Distance from Washington, D.C.: 24 miles

From I-495 (Capital Beltway): Take exit 7A, MD 5 South, toward Waldorf. In 9.5 miles MD 5 merges onto US 301 South. In 2.1 miles, turn left on Cedarville Road (see State Forest sign). In 0.3 mile, Cedarville Road veers right. In 2 miles turn right into forest entrance on Bee Oak Road. In 0.9 mile reach the visitor center parking lot and honor pay station. Trailhead GPS: N38 38.817' / W76 49.814'

THE HIKE

As the Great Depression settled over America in the 1930s, the U.S. Government started buying land rendered useless by decades of abusive farming and timbering. Faced with thousands of men without jobs and a crippled economy, Franklin Delano Roosevelt created make-work programs: the Civilian Conservation Corps (CCC) and Works Project Administration (WPA).

Spurred by the federal government, Virginia and Maryland began a program to buy abused farmland, often for pennies on the dollar. That is how Cedarville

Old charcoal kiln built by the Civilian Conservation Corps

State Forest was created. In the Coastal Plain, the government bought land that surrounded two stream valleys, Wolf Den Branch and Zekiah Swamp. They reclaimed abused farmland, planted trees, and built roads that hikers walk today beneath pine and hardwood forests.

Hiking one of those forest roads is a good time to ruminate. The path ahead is clear, and the mind wanders to what might lie off to the left and right. A gully forms alongside the road, dry in late summer. The hillside to the right steepens, and, in the crease between two hills, Wolf Den Branch gains strength.

Thanks to Cedarville State Forest, Zekiah Swamp was saved. Its headwaters originate in the forest and flow 21 miles toward the Wicomico River. Of some eighty-four streams surveyed in Maryland, Zekiah Swamp is rated the number one stronghold stream for its rare and endangered plants and animals, according to a survey by Maryland's Department of Natural Resources from 2000 to 2004.

There are two types of bogs on the East Coast: northern bogs and pocosins. The headwaters of Zekiah Swamp is classified as a northern bog. Here thrives the northern pitcher plant (*Sarracenia purpurea*), which captures insects in pools of water in its leaves, then digests them with the aid of a bacteria.

You can see an example of this rich bottomland as the trail descends alongside Wolf Den Branch. After heavy rain, the trail is washed out by a tributary that crosses it and spreads out across the flat ground. Small hummocks of grass poke out here and there, making it possible to hopscotch through the sheet flow of water. Signs of considerably more flow force can be seen in the piles of twigs and leaf debris pressed against the upstream side of trees.

In Cedarville, Zekiah Swamp wells up through the sphagnum and forms a freshwater swamp forest. The hillsides are low, and the riverbed isn't a deep channel. This is more of a spreading stream than a channelized stream. Water moves slowly, and the hiker is encouraged to move slowly as well, the better to appreciate this special scenery.

KID APPEAL

Park at Cedarville Pond, a scenic picnic area with grills and a portable toilet. Benches and picnic tables surround the pond, where Canada geese are common. It's stocked with catfish and bass, and bank fishing is allowed. Walk across the earthen dam, looking for butterflies and turtles on a nature hike short enough for even the littlest hikers. There's also the option of the 2-mile green-blazed Swamp Trail or the 2.5-mile Brown Plantation Trail, which both loop from here.

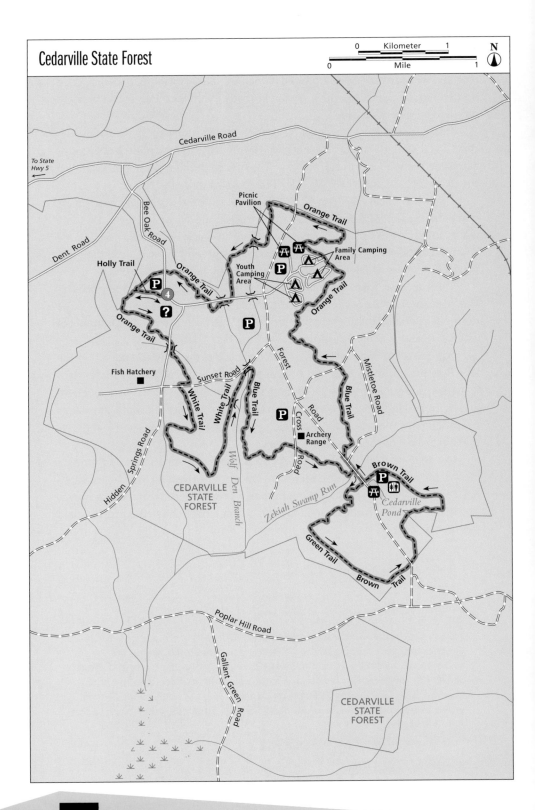

0 Kilometer 1
0 Mile 1

N

Cedarville Road

To State Hwy 5

Dent Road

Bee Oak Road

Holly Trail

Orange Trail

Picnic Pavilion

Orange Trail

Family Camping Area

Youth Camping Area

Orange Trail

Orange Trail

Fish Hatchery

Sunset Road

White Trail

White Trail

Blue Trail

Forest

Blue Trail

Mistletoe Road

Cross Road

Archery Range

Brown Trail

Cedarville Pond

Hidden Springs Road

Wolf Den Branch

CEDARVILLE STATE FOREST

Zekiah Swamp Run

Green Trail

Brown Trail

Poplar Hill Road

Gallant Green Road

CEDARVILLE STATE FOREST

MILES AND DIRECTIONS

0.0 START from a trail register at the head of Holly Trail, a single-track woods path blazed orange. Follow the trail through a forest of young holly, ash, and elm.

0.2 Turn left (south) onto Orange Trail at a T junction. (**Note:** At the end of this hike, you will approach this same junction from the right.)

0.9 Cross Hidden Springs Road, turn right (south) and walk along the shoulder. After 500 feet, turn left (east) and reenter the woods.

1.2 Bear right (south) at a fork in the trail onto white-blazed White Trail. In a few feet, turn right onto gravel Sunset Road. Walk 0.1 mile, turn left, and reenter the woods on the White Trail, a single-track dirt path through a young pine forest. (**Note:** For the next 8 miles, this route passes through an area of the forest where hunting is permitted. See *Special considerations* for more information.)

1.9 Turn left (south) onto a dirt road. In 0.1 mile, swing left (east) on White Trail.

2.4 Veer left on White Trail as it takes a northward track. After an initial climb, the trail begins a steady descent to Wolf Den Branch. (**FYI:** After heavy rains, low-elevation sections of this trail can be washed out.)

Lunch break overlooking Cedarville Pond

3.2 Stay right as White Trail merges with Sunset Road, which descends from the left. Walk 200 feet on this dirt road, then turn right onto Blue Trail, which is a single-track dirt path. In 200 feet, cross Wolf Den Branch on a footbridge. In a few feet, there is another footbridge over a wetland area. Thereafter, Blue Trail climbs to traverse a hillside offering good views down a rich stream bottomland forest.

4.2 Enter a field that appears recently timbered. Young pine saplings are starting to colonize this disturbed area.

4.3 Pass through a competitive archery range.

4.8 Turn right (south) on a gravel fire road and cross Zekiah Swamp Run. Ahead is a parking area, outhouse, and picnic areas next to Cedarville Pond.

4.9 Turn right (southwest) on Green Trail. For the next 0.5 mile, the trail swerves in and out of small gullies formed by seasonal streams that feed Zekiah Swamp Run.

6.4 Continue straight (southeast) and merge onto Brown Trail. (**Note:** Here, Green Trail turns left [north] and returns to Cedarville Pond. While it can be used as a bailout, hikers risk missing one of this loop's more scenic areas along Brown Trail.)

6.8 Descend to cross a wetlands on a wooden footbridge. This swamp, alive with frog calls and birdsong, is the headwater of Cedarville Pond and is worthy of a long break to soak in the scenery. Beyond here, the trail briefly parallels the wetlands, then climbs back into a dry forest of young hardwoods.

7.1 Turn left, continuing on Brown Trail, at a T junction with a gated forest road that fades, overgrown with grass, into the woods on the right. In 0.1 mile, turn left on Brown Trail as the old road continues straight.

7.7 Emerge from the woods at the base of Cedarville Pond. Continue straight to the gravel forest road, turn right, and cross Zekiah Swamp Run.

7.9 Turn right (north) onto Blue Trail. Within 0.1 mile, cross over Mistletoe Road, a dirt road that provides disabled hunters access. The next 1.4 miles of trail is another trip highlight: The scenic footpath winds, dips into, and rises up out of small seasonal streams under a canopy of the mixed hardwood forest.

9.1 Turn right onto the combined Orange Trail–Blue Trail.

9.3 Bear right on Orange Trail where Blue Trail splits left. Begin a climb on a gentle grade on an old dirt and gravel road that is reverting to woodsy trail.

9.9 Pass the Family Camping Area. Here, Orange Trail merges onto a dirt and gravel road. Pass two campground access roads that merge on the left; stay right at each junction. As you pass out of the camping area, there is a large fire circle on the right, and still farther, a picnic pavilion on the left.

10.1 Bear right as Orange Trail departs the camp road at a Y junction. A young pine plantation now flanks the trail on your left.

11.3 Emerge onto a power line easement and swing right. Over the next 0.1 mile, the trail alternates between the open air of the easement and the canopy of the adjacent forest, and it crosses a small stream on a footbridge.

11.9 Cross Bee Oak Road and reenter the woods directly opposite. (**Caution:** Orange Trail will cross Bea Oak Road three times in the next 0.5 mile. Watch for traffic at each crossing.)

12.5 Cross Bee Oak Road for the final time; enter the woods directly opposite.

12.7 Turn left onto Holly Trail.

13.0 HIKE ENDS at the visitor center parking area.

HIKE INFORMATION

Local information: Prince George's County, Maryland, Conference and Visitor's Bureau, Largo, MD; (301) 925-8300; (www.visitprincegeorges.com)
Good eats: Cedarville Carry Out, 1800 Cedarville Rd., Brandywine, MD; (301) 579-2888. Less than 2 miles east of the park; open 5:00 a.m. to 3:00 p.m., so you can get a hearty breakfast and pick up a sandwich for the trail.
Local outdoor stores: Beacon Surplus All-in-One Outdoor Store, 3256 Leonardtown Rd., Waldorf, MD; (301) 645-0077; www.beaconsurplus.com
Dick's Sporting Goods, 11080 Mall Circle Rd., Waldorf, MD; (301) 645-0077; www.dickssportinggoods.com
Organizations: Friends of Cedarville State Forest (FCSF), (800) 784-5380

> 🌿 **Green Tip:**
> *If you see someone else littering, muster up the courage to ask them not to.*

Cunningham Falls State Park

The views from three high points on this hike are matched only by the impressive McAfee Falls, Maryland's highest. This route, following narrow woods paths and old dirt roads that date to a bygone era of timbering and charcoal making, is designed to give hikers plenty of time to savor just how far Cunningham Falls State Park, and adjacent Catoctin Mountain Park, have come in less than one hundred years, from a denuded landscape to a small pocket of wildness.

Start: From a trailhead opposite the Manor House Visitors Center and aviary

Distance: 13.5-mile lollipop

Approximate hiking time: 6 hours

Difficulty: Difficult due to length and moderate inclines, highlighted by several strenuous but short inclines

Trail surface: Forested trails, boardwalk, open rock

Seasons: Best in winter and spring, when views are open and crowds thinned out

Other trail users: Hikers only

Handicapped accessibility: A 0.25-mile boardwalk trail provides the shortest and easiest access to Cunningham Falls. Parking lot on MD 77 is reserved for vehicles displaying the handicapped symbol.

Canine compatibility: Leashed dogs permitted on trails, except in the William Houck Area, around the lake, and on the trail to the falls

Land status: State park, national park

Fees and permits: Entrance fee

Schedule: Open daily year-round, 8:00 a.m. to dusk

Facilities: Restrooms, campground, cabins, picnic area, boat ramp, visitor center, amphitheater

Maps: DeLorme *Maryland/Delaware Atlas & Gazetteer:* Page 72 B2. USGS 7.5 minute series: *Catoctin Furnace, MD* and *Blue Ridge Summit, PA.* Custom topographic maps are sold at the Manor House Visitors Center, or online at http://dnr.maryland.gov/publiclands/trailguides.html. See also National Geographic's TOPO! software, Mid-Atlantic Region, Disc 4.

Trail contacts: Cunningham Falls State Park, 14039 Catoctin Hollow Rd., Thurmont, MD 21788; (301) 271-7574; www.dnr.state.md.us/publiclands/cunninghamguide.html

Special considerations: Fall deer hunting is permitted on 3,500 acres of undeveloped wildlands. There will be signs warning hikers, but trails generally remain open.

Finding the trailhead:
Distance from Washington, D.C.: 61 miles
From I-495 (Capital Beltway): Take I-270 north for 32 miles to Frederick, MD. Take exit 13B and get on US 15 North, a left exit. Go 12.5 miles to the park's Manor Area entrance on left. Trailhead GPS: N39 35.262' / W77 26.155'

THE HIKE

The Catoctin Trail from the Manor Area to the flat top of Bob's Hill begins as a narrow dirt footpath and, as it climbs, gradually widens to road width. Banks form on both sides, sometimes reaching as high as your head, creating a "sunken" effect. Mountain laurel is profuse in the understory of the young forest that covers the mountain slope.

Some 200 years ago, the scene would have been strikingly different. In the warmer months, a breeze would carry the pitch tar smell of a charcoal pit across the mountain. Come winter, the ax blow would ring through the forest. A horse-drawn sled laden with timber, cut into 4-foot lengths of varying widths, would trundle down this road, bringing a fresh supply for the collier (charcoal maker). A metal-lined wagon pulled by six mules would carry a load of charcoal to the blast furnace at Catoctin.

Iron furnaces operated at Catoctin from 1776 to 1903, and for the first one hundred years, were entirely fueled by charcoal, which is made from charred wood. That wood came from the vast forest that covered Catoctin Mountain. It would be hard to underemphasize the impact this industry had: Any wood made good charcoal, and so the elm, hickory, oak, and chestnut fell to the woodsman's ax. Into the twentieth century, as many as 500 men swarmed over these hills, cutting timber for railroad ties and other wooden necessities. In 1936, a former superintendent of Catoctin Mountain Park described there being "barely a tree over the size of a fence post."

The scenery is markedly different today. A young forest of hickories, elms, and other hardwoods of the Appalachian forest cover mountain slopes at lower elevations. Atop Bob's Hill and neighboring Cat Rock, thinner, well-drained soils support chestnut oaks and pitch pine.

The regeneration started in 1936, when the federal government bought 10,000 acres on Catoctin Mountain for redevelopment. Similar projects were undertaken throughout Appalachia—in

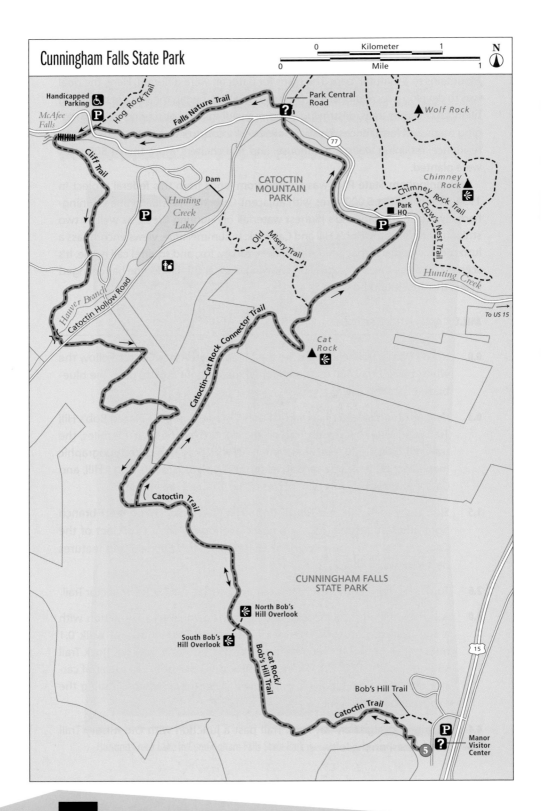

Cunningham Falls State Park

Kilometer

0 ⟶ 1

Mile

0 ⟶ 1

N

Handicapped Parking

P

McAfee Falls

Hog Rock Trail

Falls Nature Trail

Park Central Road

Wolf Rock

77

Cliff Trail

Dam

CATOCTIN MOUNTAIN PARK

Chimney Rock

Chimney Rock Trail

Hunting Creek Lake

P

Park HQ

P

Crow's Nest Trail

Old Misery Trail

Hunting Creek

Hauver Branch

Catoctin Hollow Road

Catoctin–Cat Rock Connector Trail

To US 15

Cat Rock

Catoctin Trail

CUNNINGHAM FALLS STATE PARK

15

North Bob's Hill Overlook

South Bob's Hill Overlook

Cat Rock/ Bob's Hill Trail

Bob's Hill Trail

Catoctin Trail

5

P

?

Manor Visitor Center

5.0 After a long descent, exit from Cat Rock Trail into a trailhead parking area on MD 77. At the trailboard, turn left, walk west through the parking lot, and reenter woods on an unmarked fisherman's path that parallels Little Hunting Creek beneath shady hemlocks. (**Note:** The topography will steepen on your left side and pinch the trail and creek together. At this point, look for a convenient spot to rock-hop across Little Hunting Creek, and continue the westward trek on a fisherman's path on the north stream bank.)

6.1 Climb up the north stream bank to the road shoulder of MD 77, cross the highway, and enter Catoctin Mountain Park via the paved Park Central Road. Turn left into the west parking area, walk to the far right corner, and reenter the woods on a single-track woodland trail. Within a few feet, cross a small footbridge.

7.1 Falls Nature Trail ends at a T junction with Hog Rock Trail. Turn left and descend to MD 77. On the road shoulder, turn left and walk 50 paces east, against traffic. Cross to the south side of the highway and enter a parking lot for McAfee Falls reserved for handicapped access. Inside the parking area, turn right to reach a boardwalk leading to the falls area. (**Caution:** This MD 77 crossing occurs at a blind corner for vehicles traveling in both directions.)

7.4 The boardwalk ends at an overlook of McAfee Falls. To reach the south stream bank, or to rock-scramble about the falls, retrace your footsteps along the boardwalk for 250 paces, hop off the uphill side, and follow any number of foot-worn paths to the exposed rock base of the falls. After admiring the 78-foot drop of Maryland's highest waterfall, rock-hop across Little Hunting Creek and regain the south stream bank in the area of another boardwalk overlook.

7.5 Veer right and uphill on yellow-blazed Cliff Trail. (**Note:** Lower Falls Trail [red blazes] continues straight for 0.5 mile to a parking area.)

7.7 Turn left (east) at a T junction onto blue-blazed Catoctin Trail. For 0.2 mile, Cliff and Catoctin Trails share this woodland path.

7.9 Veer right (south) on Catoctin Trail where it splits from the Cliff Trail. (**Note:** This junction is easily missed, especially in summertime when the trails are overgrown. Look for a waist-high wooden post that signals the split.)

8.3 Cross camp road (ranger station on the right). (**FYI:** There are bathrooms, a soda machine, and a freshwater spigot at the ranger station.)

8.8 Cross Catoctin Hollow Road, reenter the woods on a blue-blazed dirt foot-path, and immediately begin climbing.

10.7 Continue straight past a junction for Cat Rock Trail (yellow blazes) on the left. (**Note:** The route from here to Manor House is on the combined Catoctin/Cat Rock/Bob's Hill Trail, but only blue blazes of the Catoctin Trail are visible.)

11.8 Side trails to North and South Bob's Hill Overlooks branch left and right, respectively.

13.5 HIKE ENDS at the Manor Area Visitor Center.

OPTIONS

Cat Rock. Cross MD 77 and Little Hunting Creek and enter a parking area. Next to a wood trailboard, enter the woods on a dirt woods path. It is 1.2 miles, mostly uphill, to Cat Rock, another formation of Weaverton quartzite that rivals Chimney Rock with its ruggedness and views.

HIKE INFORMATION

Local information: Tourism Council of Frederick County, Frederick, MD; (301) 644-4047; www.fredericktourism.org

Local events/attractions: The Annual Maple Syrup demonstration takes place two weekends in March in the William Houck Area. Sausage and pancake breakfast served. Suggested donation.

Good eats: Cactus Flats, 10026 Hansonville Rd., Frederick, MD; (301) 898-3085. Just 6 miles south of the Manor Area on US 15 is a funky roadhouse stop for beer and burgers.

Local outdoor stores: The Trail House, 17 S. Market St., Frederick, MD; (301) 694-8448; www.trailhouse.com. Has hiking supplies and maps.

Hike tours: TeamLink Mountain, Frederick, MD; (301) 695-1814; www.teamlink inc.com

Organizations: Friends of Cunningham Falls State Park, Inc., 14039 Catoctin Hollow Rd., Thurmont, MD 21788

🌿 Green Tip:
All Maryland State Parks and State Forests are "trash free."
That means there are no garbage pails or waste
containers provided for visitors. Whatever trash you bring
in or find, you must take away.

Gambrill State Park

Gambrill State Park protects the lower third of the Catoctin Mountain chain. The Catoctin Trail, one of Maryland's premiere long-distance footpaths, begins here. The park and its trails date back to civic-minded residents of Frederick, Maryland, who bought the land for protection and recreation. It is a tradition that continues today with active involvement in trail maintenance by Frederick-area hikers, mountain bikers, and equestrians. At 7.4 miles, this is the longest trek that can be pieced together through the park. With so many interconnecting trails, however, options abound for making this as long or as short as time and energy permit.

Start: From the trail system parking lot on Gambrill Park Road, 0.4 mile north of the park entrance

Distance: 7.4-mile loop

Approximate hiking time: 4 hours

Difficulty: Moderate due to minimal elevation gain and well-graded trails

Trail surface: Dirt footpaths, old forest roads, gravel roads, and open-face rock

Seasons: Sept through May

Other trail users: Mountain bikers, joggers, and cross-country skiers

Handicapped accessibility: Park trails are not handicapped accessible, but the North and South Frederick Overlooks are

Canine compatibility: Leashed dogs permitted

Land status: State park

Fees and permits: None

Schedule: Apr through Oct, 8:00 a.m. to sunset; Nov through Mar, 10:00 a.m. to sunset daily

Facilities: Restrooms and picnic tables are located at the Rock Run Area. There are no restrooms at High Knob Area.

Maps: DeLorme *Maryland/ Delaware Atlas & Gazetteer:* Page 72 D2. USGS 7.5 minute series: *Middletown, MD.* See also National Geographic's TOPO! software, Mid-Atlantic Region, Disc 4. A state park–issued topographical map is available online at http://dnr .maryland.gov/publiclands/ trailguides.html.

Trail contacts: Gambrill State Park, c/o Cunningham Falls State Park, 14039 Catoctin Hollow Rd., Thurmont, MD 21788; (301) 271-7574; www.dnr.state.md.us/public lands/western/gambrill.html. The Trail House in downtown Frederick (see *Local outdoor stores*) maintains the Red Maple Trail. The Potomac Appalachian Trail Club (PATC) (Vienna, VA; www.potomac appalachian.org) maintains the Catoctin Trail and the Black Locust Trail.

THE HIKE

Half the fun of exploring a park as popular and well used as Gambrill State Park is to take every unmarked side trail in the spirit of "what if." What if this trail links up with another, and I've found a shortcut? What if I see a bear? What if . . . ?

What if you're walking uphill on a rocky footbed beneath a power line? It tops out at a grass road that swings left and continues climbing. In May, the clearing off to the left of the road is visited by wild turkeys. Farther still, the grass road rises to meet the paved road leading to a radio tower. Here, it is faster to retrace your steps back beneath the power line easement and rejoin the trail.

There are two poisonous snakes in Maryland, the northern copperhead and the timber rattler. On warm spring days, they emerge to bask in the heat of the exposed rock that mark so many overlooks and outcrops throughout Gambrill

Rattlesnake in the trail

State Park. They also like power line easements, as in the case of the timber rattler that blocked my descent back toward the Yellow Poplar Trail. Timber rattlesnakes dine on small mammals, some birds, and maybe a frog here and there. They enjoy the rocky ridgetops and forested swamps. This one seemed to prefer the rocky ridge; unwilling to budge, it forced me off trail onto a bushwhack across a dry forest of oak and hickory until I crossed paths again with Yellow Poplar Trail.

Among the highlights along this north–south route are the many wildflowers. From its trailhead, the Catoctin Trail swings north to traverse a dry forested slope. A sharp eye will catch, in the leaf litter alongside the trail, the delicate spotted wintergreen. Its serrated-edged leaves, narrow and pointed at the tip, have a white streak down the center vein that could almost pass for hand-painted. Two thin stems rise from the vortex of leaves at the base. Each stem is capped by a small yellow flower. In early spring, the stems may be red or yellow, and the buds may be closed, resembling small BB-gun–like pellets.

And just as quickly, 0.1 mile north on the trail, the dry forest upslope is covered with fiddlehead ferns. Somewhere up that slope, a seep or stream is keeping the ferns well watered.

Save for the developed overlooks at High Point, the rock outcrops and vistas are not as spectacular at Gambrill State Park as they are farther up the mountain chain at Cunningham State Park and Catoctin Mountain Park. But evidence abounds in what these three locales share: the quartzite bedrock that forms so many of the Catoctin Mountains's signature outcrops. Gambrill, together with land owned by the City of Frederick, and the state and national parks to the north, protect a beautiful woodland and significant geologic feature.

KID APPEAL

The white-blazed White Oak Trail, a 1-mile loop, is a good choice for tiny hikers. The going is easy, and no mountain bikes are allowed.

MILES AND DIRECTIONS

0.0 START from an information map board in the trail system parking area on Gambrill Park Road. Choose the Catoctin Trail/Black Locust Trail/Red Maple Trail trailhead, marked by a sign on a wooden post reading WELCOME TO THE CATOCTIN HIKING TRAIL. Walk east on this wide dirt footpath, following a triple sequence of light blue, black, and red blazes. In 300 feet past the trailhead, red-blazed Red Maple Trail splits right (south). Continue straight (east) on combined Catoctin Trail/Black Locust Trail.

0.6 Bear right (north) as Green Ash Trail merges with the Catoctin Trail.

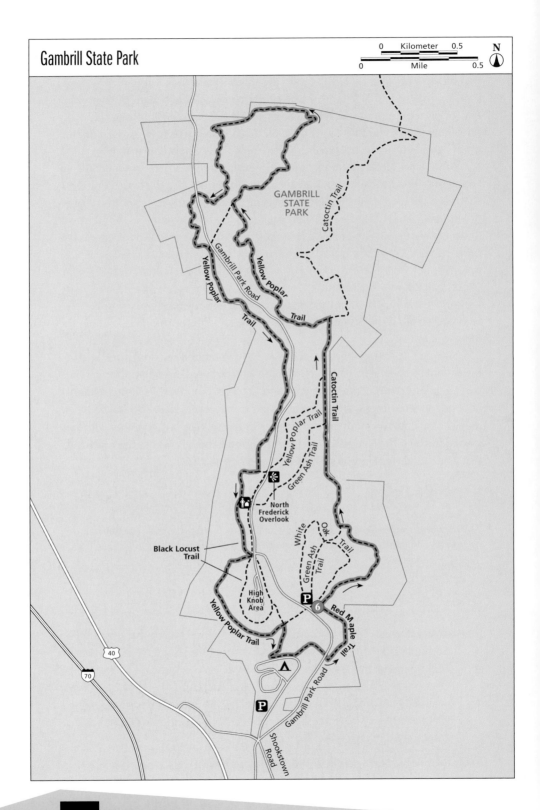

Gambrill State Park

0 Kilometer 0.5

0 Mile 0.5

N

GAMBRILL STATE PARK

Catoctin Trail

Yellow Poplar Trail

Gambrill Park Road

Yellow Poplar Trail

Catoctin Trail

Yellow Poplar Trail

Green Ash Trail

North Frederick Overlook

Black Locust Trail

White Oak Trail

Green Ash Trail

High Knob Area

Yellow Poplar Trail

P

6

Red Maple Trail

40

70

Gambrill Park Road

P

Shookstown Road

1.1 Stay straight (north) on the Catoctin Trail as Green Ash Trail and Black Locust Trail branch left to climb back to the park road.

1.3 Climb to a T junction with Yellow Poplar Trail via two switchbacks. Turn right (north) and follow combined Catoctin Trail/Yellow Poplar Trail, a wide dirt two-track road.

1.6 Catoctin Trail and Yellow Poplar Trail split at a T junction. Turn left (west) and follow yellow-blazed Yellow Poplar Trail, which is a two-track dirt road. In 0.1 mile, the route veers off the road and becomes a narrow footpath.

1.7 Cross a gravel road that links Gambrill Park Road to a radio tower. The trail reenters the woods via steps hewn from logs and rocks. An impressive set of Catoctin greenstone outcrops is visible in woods to the right.

2.1 Turn left (north) at a T junction and continue on Yellow Poplar Trail as it descends to a seasonal stream. Cross the stream and pass a pond on the right.

2.3 The trail departs the forest and follows a power line easement north. (**Note:** A sign here indicates that you've been hiking the Lower Yellow Loop.)

2.4 Turn right (northeast) at a T junction to begin the Upper Yellow Loop, which is a popular mountain bike route. (**Option:** You can shave 2 miles off this loop by turning left here and descending to Gambrill Park Road via the Lower Yellow Loop.)

Catoctin Mountain Trail runs through the park

3.2   Take a hard left (south) and avoid an unmarked footpath that continues straight (west). The trail, which is a narrow dirt footpath, soon climbs several long switchbacks through what was once an old U.S. weather station.

4.0   Cross Gambrill Park Road.

4.4   Continue straight as a spur trail branches left (this is the shortcut described in the Option at mile 2.4). As the Yellow Poplar Trail descends gently, the trail footing is rough with exposed rocks.

5.5   Turn right (west) and descend on combined Yellow Poplar/Black Locust Trail, following both yellow and black blazes. The next 0.5 mile is marked by nice wintertime views west off Catoctin Mountain. (**Side trip:** A left onto Black Locust Trail leads approximately 90 yards up to the park road and the North Frederick Overlook, which has easterly views.)

5.7   Continue straight (south) past a spur trail that branches left (east) and climbs to the park ranger station.

6.0   At a four-way trail junction, turn right (west) and follow Yellow Poplar Trail downhill on a narrow dirt footpath.

6.6   Turn right (south) on Red Maple Trail. It descends 0.1 mile to the Rock Run Area and campsites.

7.0   Cross the park road and climb the road embankment on the opposite side. A double red blaze marks your left (northeast) turn up a gravel driveway. After a brief climb, follow red blazes straight as it reenters the woods as a wide and graded path.

7.3   Turn left (west) onto the Catoctin Trail.

7.4   HIKE ENDS at the trail system parking lot.

HIKE INFORMATION

Local information: Tourism Council of Frederick County, Inc., Frederick, MD; (301) 660-2888; www.fredericktourism.org

Local events/attractions: Rose Hill Manor Park/The Children's & Farm Museum, 1611 N. Market St., Frederick, MD; (301) 600-1650; www.rosehillmuseum.com. Living-history museum interprets early American life through historic tours and events.

Good eats: John Hagen's Tavern, 5018 Old National Pike, Frederick, MD; (301) 371-9189. A historic tavern that doesn't mind customers with muddy boots. Call for directions.

Local outdoor stores: The Trail House, 17 S. Main St., Frederick, MD; (301) 694-8448; www.trailhouse.com

Great Falls Park, MD / Chesapeake and Ohio Canal National Historic Park

A public relations effort by Supreme Court Justice William O. Douglas in 1954 saved the Chesapeake and Ohio Canal and towpath from a different fate: The National Park Service had proposed paving the route as a scenic roadway on par with Skyline Drive. Instead, the towpath and canal are preserved, mostly in their original state. Between Georgetown and Great Falls, it serves as a recreational release valve for metropolitan Washington. It also makes an ideal spine for a day hike that veers off course at every opportunity to explore wooded hillsides, small stream valleys, floodplain forests, and dramatic rock cliffs overlooking the mighty Potomac River.

Start: From the Carderock Recreation Area, north parking lot
Distance: 9.1-mile loop
Approximate hiking time: 3 to 4 hours
Difficulty: Difficult due to a combination of distance, several bushwhack options, and extremely rocky, technical terrain along the Billy Goat Trail on Bear Island
Trail surface: The C&O Canal is a hard-packed dirt and stone path. Woodland dirt footpaths and old dirt mining roads characterize trails along the Gold Mine Loop. Billy Goat Trail, especially the section on Bear Island, features technical terrain across large and exposed rock faces.
Seasons: Autumn for the foliage colors, and winter for unobstructed views
Other trail users: Joggers, bicyclists, rock climbers, and kayakers (carrying their boats down to the river from Old Angler's Inn parking area)

Handicapped accessibility: Overlooks on Olmsted Island of the Potomac River at Mathers Gorge are accessible via a series of bridges and boardwalks
Canine compatibility: While generally leashed dogs are permitted, it's not practical for this described route because of the national park bans on pets on Olmsted Island, Bear Island, and "Section A" of the Billy Goat Trail
Land status: National historical park
Fees and permits: No fee required to access trails from Carderock Recreation Area
Schedule: Dawn to dusk daily. Great Falls Tavern is open daily 9:00 a.m. to 4:30 p.m. and closed on Thanksgiving, Christmas Day, and New Year's Day.
Facilities: Restrooms are located at the trailhead and Great Falls Tavern. There are picnic tables, a snack bar, visitor center, and bookstore at Great Falls Tavern.

Maps: DeLorme *Maryland/Delaware Atlas & Gazetteer:* Page 46 B2. USGS 7.5 minute series: *Falls Church, VA/MD.* Potomac Appalachian Trail Club's Map D: *Trails of the Potomac Gorge Area* available from the PATC (see *Trail contacts*).
Trail contacts: Chesapeake and Ohio Canal National Historical Park, Great Falls Tavern Visitors Center, 11710 MacArthur Blvd., Potomac, MD 20854; (301) 767-3714; www.nps.gov/choh Potomac Appalachian Trail Club (PATC), 118 Park St. SE, Vienna, VA 22210; www.potomac appalachian.org
Special considerations: Springtime flooding on the Potomac may force temporary closure of Billy Goat Trail on Bear Island with little or no advance notice. If so, finish the described route by using the C&O Canal towpath.

Finding the trailhead:

Distance from Washington, D.C.: 13 miles

From I-495 (Capital Beltway): From Maryland, take exit 41 (Carderock/Great Falls, MD) and merge directly onto Clara Barton Parkway westbound. From Virginia, take exit 41 (Clara Barton Parkway/Glen Echo), and on the exit ramp, veer left, following signs for Carderock and Clara Barton Parkway. Drive 0.9 mile on the Clara Barton Parkway and take the Carderock Recreation Area exit. Turn left at the top of the ramp, cross over the parkway, and follow the road as it sweeps right and downhill. Reach a stop sign in 0.3 mile from the parkway. Turn right (north) and drive 0.5 mile to the north parking area. The trailhead is adjacent to the bathrooms. Trailhead GPS: N38 58.570' / W77 12.344'

THE HIKE

In the woods above Great Falls, a small footpath called the Woodland Trail traverses a hillside. A few hundred feet below, walkers and bikers follow Berma Road between Old Angler's Inn parking area and Lock 16 on the C&O Canal. Here in the summertime woods, it's cool beneath a high canopy of oaks and yellow (tulip) poplars. All the signs of an active woodland community are present: hollowed-out logs, scurrying footsteps of chipmunks and squirrels on a dry, leafy forest floor. Wind rustles the leaves overhead, and there are myriad calls of songbirds.

Off to the left of the trail, there is a wide depression in the earth. Then another, then another. It looks as if someone started to dig a wide round hole, then gave up the effort, moved down the trail a bit, and started again.

These excavations—six in total spread over the first 0.1 mile of Woodland Trail after its junction with Angler Trail—are too obvious to be natural. Scattered about the edges of a few are piles of quartzite rock, milky in color and streaked with darker minerals. A healthy maple tree grows out of one depression, giving the impression that whenever these holes were made, it wasn't recently.

Legend has it that during the Civil War, a Union soldier was washing dishes in a stream nearby to these woods when a glint caught his eye. Thus was born Maryland's very own gold rush. The soldier, Private McCleary of Pennsylvania, returned after the war, bought several farms in the area, and began searching for gold. Rumors of his activity spread. The first mine shaft was sunk in 1867.

In all, some twenty-one mines operated in the Great Falls area in Maryland. The most successful mines were those that struck gold-bearing quartz veins. Exploratory trenches were dug to locate these veins, and horizontal tunnels, called adits, were drilled into hillsides. The largest mine, Maryland Mine, operated sporadically

KID APPEAL

A stable of about six mules pull the C&O Canal boat rides, much like they did in the 1870s. The mules all have names and unique personalities. When not working the eight-month season on the canal, they relax at George Washington's Mount Vernon in Alexandria, Virginia. Mules—actually a cross between a horse and a donkey—were the "engines" of the C&O Canal boats, as explained by costumed park interpreters on board the boat rides. Children were usually the mule drivers, and the mules became their pets and companions.

Out-fall at Great Falls Tavern

Great Falls Park, MD/Chesapeake and Ohio Canal NHP

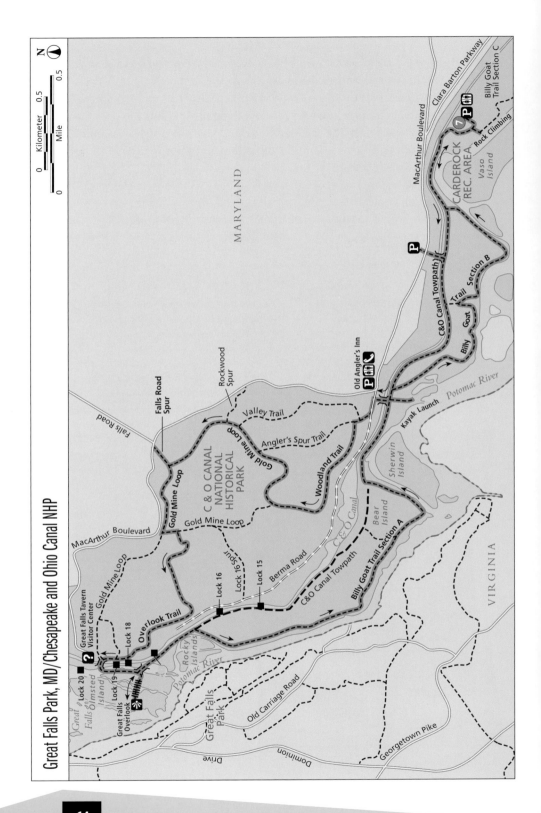

N

Kilometer
0   0.5

0   0.5
Mile

MARYLAND

C & O CANAL NATIONAL HISTORICAL PARK

Falls Road

Falls Road Spur

Rockwood Spur

Valley Trail

Angler's Spur Trail

Gold Mine Loop

Woodland Trail

MacArthur Boulevard

Gold Mine Loop

Gold Mine Loop

Old Angler's Inn

Lock 16

Lock 16½

Lock 15

Berma Road

Overlook Trail

Lock 18

Lock 19

Lock 20

Great Falls Tavern Visitor Center

Great Falls Overlook

Great Olmsted Falls Island

Rocky Islands

Potomac River

Great Falls Park

Old Carriage Road

Dominion Drive

Georgetown Pike

VIRGINIA

C&O Canal

Bear Island

Billy Goat Trail Section A

C&O Canal Towpath

Sherwin Island

Kayak Launch

Potomac River

C&O Canal Towpath

Billy Goat Trail Section B

Billy Goat Trail

MacArthur Boulevard

Clara Barton Parkway

CARDEROCK REC. AREA

Vaso Island

Rock Climbing

Billy Goat Trail Section C

7

from 1900 to 1939, and evidence of its existence remains: vertical shafts as deep as 100 feet in the hillside that hikers can explore via the Gold Mine Loop Trail. Maryland was also the most successful mine. It operated a mill for crushing extracted ore, a blacksmith shop, an assay office, and a water tower. Average yield, according to park interpretive material, was a half ounce of gold per ton of hard quartz.

Hikers can still see the Maryland Mine's old water tower (rebuilt by the park service) via a spur trail that links the Gold Mine Loop with Falls Road. The mine shafts are filled in and fenced off, leaving those small swales alongside the Woodland Trail as tantalizing clues to this era of speculation that ended in 1940. Official records of the U.S. Mint record some 5,000 ounces of gold from all of Maryland's mining activity, the majority coming from these hillsides.

MILES AND DIRECTIONS

0.0 START from the north parking area of the Carderock Recreation Area. Walk past the bathrooms on a concrete path that becomes a dirt path. Cross a boardwalk over low terrain that may be wet in the rainy seasons, and reach a T junction with blue-blazed Billy Goat Trail. (**FYI:** The rocks before you are the top of a 60-foot-high riverside bluff known to climbers as Jungle Cliff and Hades Heights. In the evening and on weekends, it is crawling with climbers setting up top rope anchors and testing their skills on well-worn routes.)

0.05 Turn right (north) on Billy Goat Trail. As you walk through the woodland, watch for a double blue blaze, where you veer right to avoid a climber's path down to the base of the rocks.

0.1 Emerge from the woods onto the C&O Canal towpath. Turn left (north).

0.5 Pass a junction on the left for the Billy Goat Trail. Continue straight on the towpath. (**Note:** The trail left is the return portion of this route.)

1.5 Turn right and cross the C&O Canal on a footbridge that leads to the Old Angler's Inn parking area. Climb a set of rough-hewn steps to the lower parking lot. Look left and locate a set of wood stairs near the chemical toilets (the stairs have a track alongside them for pushing a bicycle uphill). Climb and, at the top, turn left onto Berma Road.

1.6 Reach a sewer facility surrounded by a chain link fence. Trace the fence around and behind the facility. Look for a dirt path that enters the woods and reaches the signed junction of Valley Trail and Angler's Spur Trail. Veer left at this forked junction and climb on the Angler's Spur Trail.

1.7 Turn left (north) onto the Woodland Trail, a single-track woods path.

6.1 Pass Purplehorse Beach, a small cove and sandbar at the river's edge.

6.2 Bear left (southeast) as the trail splits around a steep rock formation. (**Note:** The right fork rejoins Billy Goat Trail after taking a more difficult route over the rock promontory.)

6.3 Sweep around a pond on your right and descend to cross a stream. (**Bailout:** After crossing the stream, look for an unmarked path that turns left [east]. Follow this back to the towpath if you've had enough of uneven terrain and difficult trekking over open rock.)

6.5 Reach a final overlook onto the Potomac. On the shore opposite, Difficult Run is visible. Follow the trail as it sweeps left (east). In the next 0.1 mile, descend steeply to cross a stream, climb the opposite bank, and skirt a channel that divides Bear Island from Sherwin Island to the south.

6.8 Reach a junction with the C&O Canal towpath. Turn right (south).

7.2 Stay straight past a bridge to the Old Angler's Inn parking area.

7.3 Turn right (south) on blue-blazed Billy Goat Trail (Section B). The trail is a narrow footpath that is less technical than Section A. (**FYI:** For views over the Potomac, follow any one of a number of unmarked footpaths that lead to rock outcrops.)

Canal boat ride

7.8 Turn right and descend to the river's edge. Climb steeply up and between large boulders. (**Caution:** The trail here is not self-evident, and it takes some scouting to locate the blue blazes. Watch your footing.)

8.0 Swing left into a stream gully. Cross on the large boulders, turn right, and follow the trail back to the river's edge.

8.6 Reach a junction with the C&O Canal towpath. Turn right (south) onto the towpath.

9.0 Turn right (west) onto Billy Goat Trail (Section C).

9.1 HIKE ENDS at the north parking area of the Carderock Recreation Area.

HIKE INFORMATION

Local information: Montgomery County Visitors Information Center, 12900 Middlebrook Road, Suite 1400, Germantown, MD; (301) 916-0698; www.cvb montco.com

Good eats: Old Angler's Inn, 10801 MacArthur Blvd., Potomac, MD; (301) 365-2425; www.oldanglersinn.com. Reservations and business casual attire.

Irish Inn at Glen Echo, 6119 Tulane Ave., Glen Echo, MD; (301) 229-6600; www .irishinnglenecho.com. Located at the corner of Tulane Avenue and MacArthur Boulevard in Glen Echo. More casual atmosphere than Old Angler's Inn.

Local outdoor stores: REI, 1701 Rockville Pike, Rockville, MD; (301) 230-7670; www.rei.com

Hudson Trail Outfitters, 401 N. Frederick Ave., Gaithersburg, MD; (301) 948-2474; www.hudsontrail.com

Dick's Sporting Goods, 2 Grand Corner Ave., Gaithersburg, MD; (301) 947-0200; www.dickssportinggoods.com

Hike tours: C&O Canal park rangers lead weekly hikes. Check with the Great Falls Tavern Visitors Center for schedules.

Organizations: C&O Canal Association, Glen Echo, MD; (301) 983-0825; www .candocanal.org

The Nature Conservancy, Maryland/D.C. Field Office, Bethesda, MD; (301) 897-8570; www.tnc.org

Potomac Conservancy, Silver Spring, MD; (301) 608-1188; www.potomac.org

> 🌿 **Green Tip:**
> *If you're toting food, leave the packaging at home. Repack your provisions in ziplock bags that you can re-use and that can double as garbage bags on the way out of the woods.*

Birdlife fluctuates seasonally as well. It is said that 25,000 waterfowl descend on the more than 4,000 protected acres around Jug Bay. (In addition to this nature preserve, there is a wildlife sanctuary to the south, and another across the river in Anne Arundel County.) Tundra swans, Canada geese, and green-winged teal winter over. In fall, tens of thousands of sora rails flock here during migration. They seek grains of northern wild rice, which is more abundant here than anywhere else in all of the Chesapeake Bay's freshwater estuarine reaches. It's this plant that so preoccupies scientists and researchers who use Jug Bay as a kind of outdoor laboratory to study marsh ecosystems, birds, and plant life. For while the sora loves the seed head, with its long black grains that congregate in a bushy head, ducks and Canada geese love the stems and roots. Researchers responded by fencing the biggest stands of wild rice and removed the offending geese, so to favor the sora.

Sora belong to the genus *Gruiforms*, and together the six species form a fascinating aspect of any marsh ecosystem. Their call is a harsh, repetitious series, with variety between the six species in pitch and tone. All of them, however, call in a series of five or six, with the last few calls tailing off to silence. One call can set off six, ten, or even twenty other rails in the vicinity, resulting in a cacophony. It is unforgettable, and a bit mysterious given that the bird is rarely seen, hunkered down in the thick vegetation.

Birdwatching on Jug Bay

MILES AND DIRECTIONS

0.0 START on a dirt road that heads downhill opposite the visitor center. Before reaching the bottom, veer left (south) onto Black Walnut Creek Nature Trail. Over the next 0.2 mile, this trail, marked by black arrows on white sticks, will descend to and cross Black Walnut Creek via a boardwalk.

0.2 Bear left at a fork in the boardwalk. (**Note:** The right fork leads to an observation platform overlooking Black Walnut Creek.) Within a few feet after this split, the boardwalk ends. Bear left again when a dirt footpath forks right.

0.3 Bear left (east) on a boardwalk leading to an observation blind overlooking Jug Bay. After visiting the blind, return to the Black Walnut Creek Nature Trail, turn left (south), and climb a short, steep hill. At the top, turn left (south) again and follow Green Trail, which is an old dirt forest road. (**Note:** This trail is multiuse for horseback riding.)

0.9 Stay straight (south) and merge onto Brown Trail at an intersection where Green Trail turns right.

1.3 Reach the end of the Brown Trail at an overlook of the Patuxent River shaded by a large oak tree. Return to Green Trail.

1.6 Turn left (west) on Green Trail.

2.2 Turn right (north) on Red Trail. (**Note:** A left on Red Trail leads to the park's southern trails, which can add as many as 4 miles to a day's hike.)

2.5 Cross Park Entrance Road. Two posts mark where the Red Trail reenters the woods.

3.1 Turn right (east) onto an unmarked, but clear, dirt trail. It swings south, parallels Red Trail for a few hundred yards, merges with Purple Trail, and swings east to follow the edge of a loblolly pine tree plantation.

3.5 As the trail passes through a forest of young maples and sweetgum, notice on the right the headwaters of Black Walnut Creek.

4.0 Turn right (east) and walk alongside the paved Park Entrance Road.

4.5 HIKE ENDS at the visitor center.

Leaving the Little Patuxent behind, you enter a mixed pine and hardwood forest on the 2.5-mile Forest Habitats Nature Trail. Here, there is a chance to delve deeper into the woodland environment. Elevation loss/gain is minimal, although the trail does a nice job of riding a small knoll before dropping down into a stream valley. A fox may leave its scat strategically in the middle of the dirt trail, a reminder that something other than humans lays stake to this ground. From somewhere deep into the pines, an unseen northern cardinal calls *tic-tic-tic* from its perch. If you're walking in springtime, linger beneath the canopy of mature American beech trees. You may feel a light brushing on your skin, like raindrops. It's the tiny scales from the beech's thornlike buds that have peeled away and fallen.

The American beech in many ways symbolizes woodland hikes in the Coastal Plain region of Maryland and Virginia. It is everywhere: as a skinny-trunked tree in the understory of larger sweetgums and tulip poplars or as a large, broad-trunked specimen in the forest canopy. Its tight gray bark splits as the tree grows larger; the

---

KID APPEAL

Start in the visitor center. Press "play" on an MP3 player to hear ten wildlife sounds, from a turkey vulture to a red fox. In a small aquarium, meet Frank, an eastern painted turtle, and Stinky, an aptly named musk turtle.

Forest Habitats Nature Trail

tree is an oft-preferred canvas for young lovers with pen knives. Its light tan leaves linger on the branch throughout winter, only to be pushed off by new buds come spring. Where they grow in clusters, it's likely that the beech are of the same family; this tree sends out rhizomes, or undergrown stems, that send up sucker shoots that grow into full-blown trees. Each sucker is genetically a clone of the mother tree.

Beech trees share a trait of one of the most inconspicuous plants of a wet forest: the club moss. Ground pine, a type of club moss, is evident along the Forest Habitats Nature Trail after it descends off a hill and parallels a seasonal stream. At a glance, it looks like a dollhouse-size pine tree. It is a marker plant, in that it can tell you how old (or young) a forest is. Rarely do you find ground pine in a forest more than fifty years old. As tiny as they are, they share something in common with the beech trees upslope a few feet away: They replicate themselves via underground stems and suckers that rise up a few inches away. Biologists say that in prehistoric time, the small ground pine grew to more than 100 feet high. Its spores and decaying vegetation formed coal that we have mined for more than a century. Today, this inconspicuous ground cover is a chance to appreciate that in small things, there are big stories.

OPTIONS

The South Tract of the refuge is home to the National Wildlife Refuge Visitor Center and Cash Lake.

HIKE INFORMATION

Local information: Prince George's County Conference and Visitor's Bureau, 9200 Basil Court, Largo, MD; (301) 925-8300; www.co.pg.md.us

Local events/attractions: Patuxent Wildlife Festival, National Wildlife Visitor Center, 10901 Scarlet Tanager Loop, Laurel, MD; (301) 497-5763; http://patuxent .fws.gov. Annual autumn festival marks National Wildlife Refuge Week. Live animals, kids' activities, tours of the USGS Patuxent Wildlife Research Center.

Patuxent: NWR Headquarters

In the world of wildlife biology, Patuxent's name stands out for another reason. The refuge's Central Tract (off-limits to general public) is the administrative and research headquarters for our National Wildlife Refuge system— the nerve center for the 550 refuges in America. This is a clearinghouse for research data and administrative rulings, where hard science gathered in far-flung places like the Florida Everglades and the Alaskan arctic is stored. Bird-banding studies alone represent more than eight million records (and counting) dating back to the early twentieth century.

1.2 Enter a power line easement, turn left (south), and reenter the woods. Ahead, the trail will skirt this easement once more before delving back into the woods.

1.9 Stay straight as an unmarked trail crosses Perimeter Trail going right and left. Over the next 0.2 mile, Perimeter Trail will cross this same path twice more. (**FYI:** Perimeter Trail was built and is maintained by MORE, a mountain bike club. Bike riders dig this ribbon-candy–like trail pattern, even if it sometimes drives hikers up a wall [or a tree]!)

2.2 Bear left (south) onto a road that merges from the right. In forty steps, split left (east) off the road back into the woods.

2.3 An old gray barn looms like a ghost through the trees off the right side of the trail. There's a rusted farm tractor on the trailside.

2.4 Make a hard left (south) as Perimeter Trail merges with a dirt road that enters from the right. Immediately, cross a footbridge over a stream, and begin a long climb on an old road.

2.7 After skirting a pine plantation—with sounds from US 301 audible on the left—Perimeter Trail reenters the canopy of woods and swings hard to the right (north).

Old barn

Mushrooms on a nurse log

2.9   Cross straight across a power line easement and reenter woods.

3.3   Stay straight (east) as an old overgrown road splits right (south) off Perimeter Trail. In 0.2 mile, this road intersects Perimeter Trail again.

3.9   Cross straight across a road and reenter the woods, descending on a narrow footpath.

4.4   Cross straight over a blacktop road and reenter the woods. (**FYI:** This blacktop road is the private drive to historic Mount Airy, which is closed to the general public but may be reserved for special events.)

There are a dozen types of frogs, fourteen types of snakes, and dozens of species of dragonflies and damselflies in the refuge.

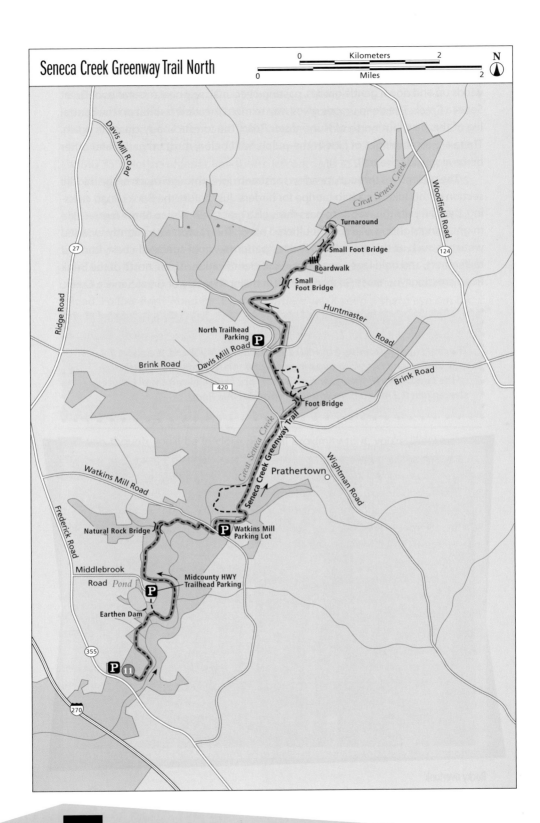

Kilometers
0   2
0   2
Miles

N

Great Seneca Creek

Davis Mill Road

27

Woodfield Road

124

Turnaround

Small Foot Bridge

Boardwalk

Small Foot Bridge

Huntmaster Road

North Trailhead Parking

Ridge Road

Brink Road   Davis Mill Road

420

Brink Road

Foot Bridge

Great Seneca Creek

Watkins Mill Road

Prathertown

Wightman Road

Seneca Creek Greenway Trail

Natural Rock Bridge

Watkins Mill Parking Lot

Frederick Road

Middlebrook Road   Pond

Midcounty HWY Trailhead Parking

Earthen Dam

355

11

270

and enter a field. By midsummer, the grass is waist high, and bird-watching is in high gear. Sightings include indigo bunting, red-eyed vireo, and scarlet tanager.

Great Seneca Creek's watershed lies entirely within Montgomery County, and the stream's health is intrinsically tied to the surrounding community. There are large communities—Montgomery Village and Gaithersburg—and adjoining farmland is being developed for homes. Three wastewater treatment plants discharge into tributaries of Great Seneca, yet in spite of all this, the stream is cited by the county as being well stocked with fish, from coldwater species near its headwaters to smallmouth bass farther south.

From the trail, the stream's character varies from a wide, broad waterway to a narrow and winding creek, especially north of Huntmaster Road. There are no waterfalls, but rather riffles and small rapids formed by stream rocks. At particularly sharp bends, the creek carves out the inside corner, leaving a sheer wall of sand. Tree roots uncovered by the erosion stick out from the bank, and where the cut is particularly fast and deep, a tree's foothold will weaken, and it leans over the stream.

The river bends offer another place to explore, on small bars where the moving water has deposited piles of sand. Here, the amateur tracker can scan the soft mud for clues of past visitors and their tracks. Canada geese tracks are webbed, while the great blue heron leaves a wide track showing three talonlike claws. There may be the dainty footprints of a raccoon or the deep imprint of a deer.

MILES AND DIRECTIONS

0.0 START from a trailboard in the parking lot on MD 355. Walk around the trailboard and down a grass slope. Follow a gravel path that veers left (north) into the woods. En route, you will pass a small brown trail sign that reads SENECA CREEK GT TO MIDCOUNTY HWY TRAIL PARKING. There are light blue blazes on the tree. Within 100 yards, the trail splits. Turn left and continue north on the Seneca Creek Greenway Trail (GT), which is now a dirt footpath.

0.5 After a brief climb, swing right (north) to stay on the Seneca Creek GT to avoid an unmarked trail that branches left.

0.9 Pass an outfall from a pond formed by a large earthen dam that is up the hill on your left. After rock-hopping across the outfall stream, veer right at a junction with a spur trail on the left that leads to the Midcounty Highway trailhead parking lot.

1.4 After a short but steep climb, linger for a moment at a rock outcrop that offers a wonderful perch and view down into the stream valley. The Seneca Creek GT continues north from this outcrop.

1.8 Continue straight on the Seneca Creek GT where another dirt footpath branches left, leading to the Midcounty Highway.

2.6 Cross Rock Bridge, a natural stone bridge over a tributary of Great Seneca Creek.

2.8 Emerge from the woods onto a paved road. Turn left (north) and climb the paved road to Watkins Mill Road. Turn right (east), walk cross Great Seneca Creek via the Watkins Mill Road highway bridge. On the other side, turn left and cross Watkins Road to its north side.

3.0 Pass through the Watkins Mill parking lot and continue north on the Seneca Creek GT. Here, a single-track dirt path sweeps to the right and passes an electrical substation on the left side of the trail.

3.3 Cross a small tributary stream on a footbridge and, in about 10 feet, swing left on the Seneca Creek GT to avoid an unmarked trail that goes straight and uphill. (**Note:** Over the next 0.4 mile, numerous foot trails intersect with Seneca Creek GT. None are blazed, while the Seneca Creek GT itself is clearly marked with blue blazes.)

Stream crossing at the north end of Seneca Creek Greenway Trail

3.6 As you descend back into the stream valley, stay straight on Seneca Creek GT at a junction with an unmarked trail on the left. (**Bailout:** Turn left [south] and follow the unmarked trail as it doubles back alongside the stream to rejoin Seneca Creek GT in 0.7 mile. It is another 3.3 miles back to the MD 355 trail parking lot, for a 7.6-mile round-trip.)

4.3 Reach a trailboard at the junction of Wightman and Brink Roads. Cross straight over Wightman, turn left, walk to the corner, and cross Brink Road. Follow the Seneca Creek GT as it skirts the edge of woods on your left and the lawn of a private residence visible on the right.

4.45 Reenter the woods on the Seneca Creek GT.

4.5 Cross a large footbridge over a tributary of Great Seneca Creek. Ahead, veer left (north) as the trail passes over flat terrain of a streamside field.

4.8 A mowed path splits right off Seneca Creek GT and heads for the hillside woods. Continue straight on blue-blazed Seneca Creek GT and enter the woods. (**Bailout:** Veer right on the mowed path and climb the wooded hillside. In 0.1 mile, turn right on a woodland path. This trail becomes a wide grassy road and swings left to descend to the Seneca Creek GT near the bridge you crossed at 4.5 miles. Follow the trail south and return to the MD 355 trailhead parking lot for a 10-mile round-trip.)

5.2 Cross straight over Huntmaster Road. From here north, Seneca Creek GT takes on deep-woods character as you cross hilly terrain overlooking Great Seneca Creek.

6.3 Seneca Creek GT merges with a utility easement marked by orange pipes sticking straight up. Follow the trail's narrow dirt footpath through tall grass. Ahead, stay alert as the Seneca Creek GT takes a hard right (east) to thread a thin buffer between the easement and private property on your right.

6.5 Seneca Creek GT takes a brief detour into the woods to cross a tributary stream of Great Seneca Creek. Reemerge onto the utility easement and cross straight over. The easement continues uphill off to the right, while the creek is far downhill on your left.

Historic gristmills were located on Seneca Creek from the colonial period to the early twentieth century. Watkins Mill was a gristmill and sawmill located on the south side of Watkins Mill Road. Ruins of Davis Mill can be seen upstream of the northern trailhead. A third mill, the Middleton Mill, was located near the MD 355 bridge.

6.9 Reach Great Seneca Creek at a stream crossing with large stepping-stone rocks. This is the northern end of the Seneca Creek GT. Retrace the trail back to Huntmaster Road.

8.6 Return to Huntmaster Road. (**Options:** If you're hiking this as a point-to-point, turn right and follow the paved road 0.1 mile downhill to cross Great Seneca Creek on a road bridge. The parking area is immediately after the bridge, on the right, at the junction of Huntmaster and Davis Mill Roads. If you are hiking this route as an out-and-back, cross straight over Huntmaster Road and reenter the woods.)

13.8 HIKE ENDS at the MD 355 trailhead parking area.

OPTIONS

The Lower Magruder Trail links to the Seneca Creek GT at its northern end. By crossing the stream and continuing north, you'll follow first Great Seneca Creek, and then veer northwest to follow Magruder Branch. In 3.3 miles, the trail enters Damascus Recreational Park. There are future plans to link Seneca Creek GT to Patuxent State Park to the north, which will create a 25-mile-long stream valley trail from the Patuxent to the Potomac.

HIKE INFORMATION

Local information: Montgomery County Visitors Information Center, 12900 Middlebrook Road, Suite 1400, Germantown, MD; (301) 916-0698; www.cvbmontco.com

Good eats: Middlebrook Restaurant, 19201 Frederick Road, Germantown, MD; (301) 428-0263

Dogfish Head Alehouse, 800 West Diamond Ave., Gaithersburg, MD; (301) 963-4847

Local outdoor stores: REI, 1701 Rockville Pike, Rockville, MD; (301) 230-7670; www.rei.com

Hudson Trail Outfitters, 401 N. Frederick Ave., Gaithersburg, MD; (301) 948-2474; www.hudsontrail.com

Dick's Sporting Goods, 2 Grand Corner Ave., Gaithersburg, MD; (301) 947-0200; www.dickssportinggoods.com

Organizations: Seneca Creek Greenway Trail Coalition, www.senecatrail.info. Offers volunteer opportunities for helping maintain and patrol trail sections.

Seneca Creek Greenway Trail South (#2)

This lower leg of the 25-mile Seneca Creek Greenway Trail, from River Road to Black Rock Mill, sees less foot traffic than either the middle or northern sections. Consequently, its gentle mix of woods and meadows offers hikers hours of walking time with few interruptions. Seneca Creek State Park manages a portion of this trail and its handiwork is noticeable as you pass through fields planted with row upon row of sycamore saplings. Bookending the nature walk are two relics of history, an old mill, and a restored lock house on the C&O Canal.

Start: From a trail sign on Seneca Road

Distance: 6.5-mile point-to-point

Approximate hiking time: 2.5 hours

Difficulty: Moderate due to steep hill climbs where the stream valley narrows. Otherwise, the trails are well marked and maintained, and crossovers of state and county roads are easy to follow.

Trail surface: Paved road and sidewalks, dirt footpaths, fields and meadows

Seasons: Best in all seasons

Other trail users: Equestrians permitted on the trail between Berryville Road and MD 28

Canine compatibility: Leashed dogs permitted

Land status: State park

Fees and permits: None

Schedule: Open daily dawn to dusk. See *Options* for tours of Riley's Lockhouse in nearby C&O Canal National Historic Park.

Facilities: There are bathrooms in Seneca Landing Park on Riley's Lock Road. To reach them from the southern trailhead, walk down Seneca Road to River Road, cross straight over, and follow Riley's Lock Road south. Bathrooms are on the left in a parking area within 0.5 mile. (*Note:* At the end of this 0.7-mile dead-end road is Riley's Lockhouse and the Seneca Aqueduct, both part of the C&O Canal Park. See *Options*.)

Maps: DeLorme *Maryland/Delaware Atlas & Gazetteer:* Page 54 (inset) D2. USGS 7.5-minute series: *Seneca, MD/VA* and *Germantown, MD*. A waterproof topographic map of Seneca Creek State Park trails is available online at http://dnr.maryland.gov/publiclands/trailguides.html or by mail from the Maryland Department of Natural Resources,

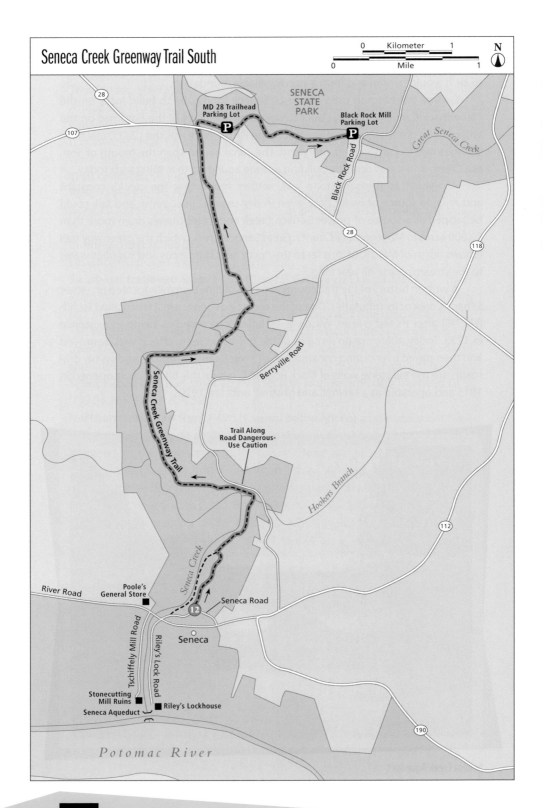

Seneca Creek Greenway Trail South

0   Kilometer   1
0   Mile   1

N

SENECA STATE PARK

MD 28 Trailhead Parking Lot

Black Rock Mill Parking Lot

Black Rock Road

Great Seneca Creek

28

107

28

118

Berryville Road

Seneca Creek Greenway Trail

Trail Along Road Dangerous- Use Caution

Hookers Branch

112

Seneca Creek

River Road

Poole's General Store

Seneca Road

12

Seneca

Tschiffely Mill Road

Riley's Lock Road

Stonecutting Mill Ruins

Seneca Aqueduct

Riley's Lockhouse

190

Potomac River

> *The name Seneca derives from the Native Americans who hunted and camped along this stream valley. Early charts show the name as "Sinegar Cr." Its translation from the Algonquin-speaking Senecas is likely "Stony Creek," an apt description for the quality red sandstone mined nearby.*

Black Rock Mill's imposing edifice is but one reminder of many of the human activity in the stream valley. There is a small farmer's pond downhill from the trail near its southern trailhead on Seneca Road. In spring, this small depression is teeming with frogs and toads. Close inspection finds wetland plants like skunk cabbage prominent near a small spring that trickles off the hillside. The jack-in-the-pulpit wildflower grows here, too, and is worth getting down on hands and knees for a closer look. The flower looks like it has a hood, but closer inspection shows that its floral spike, called a spadix, is wrapped in a sheath that then curves over the flower. The spadix is the "jack," and the sheath, also called a spathe, is the "pulpit."

"Indian turnip" is an old nickname for jack-in-the-pulpit, reference to its tuber-like root used by Native Americans as a food source. The period when this plant was valued as a food source is gone, but like Seneca Creek and the greenway trail, its value now lies in its natural beauty and the pleasure it brings to those of us who like a few hours of quiet woodland walking.

MILES AND DIRECTIONS

0.0 START from the Seneca Creek Greenway Trail (GT) trailhead on Seneca Road. There is a trail sign that gives mileage to Berryville Road. Enter the woods on a blue-blazed dirt footpath that traces a hillside above an old farmer's pond—now a vibrant wetlands alive with frog and bird calls—downhill on the left.

0.4 Veer right (north) at a V junction in the Seneca Creek GT. (**Note:** The trail that merges from the left is also marked with blue blazes; it is a low-country route leading left [south] to Seneca Road via the streamside in 0.5 mile.)

1.0 After a long climb, the trail levels briefly, then descends toward Berryville Road.

> ### KID APPEAL
>
> *Short length and easy terrain make this a perfect weekend day hike for the youngster. You can add a history lesson by spending time at the Black Rock Mill (northern trailhead) and Riley's Lockhouse on the C&O Canal (near the southern trailhead).*

OPTIONS

Walk 0.7 mile south of the southern trailhead to visit Riley's Lockhouse on the C&O Canal. From the trailhead, follow Seneca Road south to where it intersects with River Road. Cross straight over River Road and follow paved Riley's Lock Road through a county park to reach the lock house. Here, too, is the famous Seneca Aqueduct, one of eleven built along the canal to bridge the mouths of large streams.

HIKE INFORMATION

Local information: Montgomery County Visitors Information Center, 12900 Middlebrook Road, Suite 1400, Germantown, MD; (301) 916-0698; www.cvbmontco .com

Local events/attractions: Girl Scouts dressed in nineteenth-century period garb offer guided tours of Riley's Lockhouse (see *Options*) on Sat and Sun spring through fall. Call the C&O Canal National Historic Park's visitor center at Great Falls Tavern (301-767-3714) on a Thurs or Fri to learn if tours are offered that weekend.

Calleva, 13015 Riley's Lock Road, Poolesville, MD; (301) 216-1248; www.calleva .org. An outdoor adventure company based on Seneca Creek near Riley's Lockhouse. Introduction to kayaking and canoeing, white-water rafting, rock climbing, ropes courses, biking, and more, geared for parties, school groups, and corporate outings.

Good eats: Poole's General Store, 16315 Old River Road, Seneca, MD; (301) 948-5372. A feed and hardware store with sandwiches, drinks, and a small picnic area.

At the Darnesville crossroads, 2.7 miles north of the trailhead on MD 112/Seneca Road, you'll find a supermarket and gas station.

Local outdoor stores: REI, 1701 Rockville Pike, Rockville, MD; (301) 230-7670; www.rei.com

Hudson Trail Outfitters, 401 N. Frederick Ave., Gaithersburg, MD; (301) 948-2474; www.hudsontrail.com

Dick's Sporting Goods, 2 Grand Corner Ave., Gaithersburg, MD; (301) 947-0200; www.dickssportinggoods.com

Organizations: Friends of Seneca Creek State Park, Gaithersburg, MD; (301) 924-2127; www.dnr.maryland.gov/publiclands/central/senecafriendsof.html

Seneca Creek Greenway Trail Coalition, www.senecatrail.info

Sugarloaf Mountain

A solitary mountain surrounded by flat Piedmont farmland, Sugarloaf Mountain stands out in more ways than one. It is a beacon for outdoors enthusiasts in the Greater Washington, D.C., area, drawing an estimated quarter of a million people annually who hike, horseback ride, and mountain bike. Its forests are flush with wild-flowers in spring and songbirds throughout summer. Upon its heights, views stretch to the Blue Ridge, the Potomac River, and beyond. Miles of trails can be linked into outings as short as a few hours or as long as a full day. We designed this route to capture as many viewpoints as possible, starting with the peak and stretching to the park's remote northern ridges. The length is modest, but the rewards are ample.

Start: From the East View Overlook parking area

Distance: 5.9-mile loop

Approximate hiking time: 3 hours

Difficulty: Moderate due to several short, but very steep, climbs. There is some open rock terrain and some eroded sections of steep trail where footing may be difficult.

Trail surface: Forested trails, open rock face, and old forest roads

Seasons: May through Oct

Other trail users: Horses are permitted on the Yellow Trail only. Mountain bikes are permitted on the Yellow Trail only between Memorial Day and Labor Day, Mon through Fri.

Handicapped accessibility: Trails are not accessible, but the East View and West View Overlook parking areas offer panoramas across the surrounding countryside

Canine compatibility: Leashed dogs permitted

Land status: Private land conservancy

Fees and permits: None

Schedule: Daily 8:00 a.m. to 1 hour before sunset

Facilities: Portable toilets, picnic tables, and drinking water at the main entrance gate. A historic mansion and formal gardens can be rented for special events.

Maps: DeLorme *Maryland/Dela-ware Atlas & Gazetteer:* Page 55 C6. USGS 7.5 minute series: *Buckeys-town, MD/VA.* You can download the park's own line-drawn trail map at www.sugarloafmd.com. That same map is available at the park entrance on Comus Road.
Trail contacts: Stronghold, Incorporated, 7901 Comus Rd., Dickerson, MD 20842; (703) 499-9696;

www.sugarloafmd.com
Special considerations: Timber rattlesnakes and copperheads, both poisonous snakes, are found on Sugarloaf Mountain. They prefer open rock areas and small caves. Use caution when exploring around the peak, as well as at White Rocks on the Northern Peaks Trail.

Finding the trailhead:
Distance from Washington, D.C.: 42 miles
From I-270: Take exit 22, the Barnesville and Hyattstown exit, which is also marked as the exit for Sugarloaf Mountain. At the bottom of the ramp, merge onto MD 109 South and follow it for 2.9 miles. In the crossroads community of Comus, turn right onto MD 95 (the turn is marked by the Comus Inn). Drive another 2.3 miles to Stronghold, a wide spot in the road at a four-way intersection. As you enter this intersection, veer right and pass through the gated boundary of Sugarloaf Mountain Preserve. Follow this paved road between two barns, and then uphill for 2 miles to the East View Overlook parking area. Trailhead GPS: N39 15.632' / W77 23.406'

THE HIKE

On the short, steep climb to Sugarloaf's summit from East View Overlook parking area, soil underfoot is thin and flinty, laced with small white stone chips. They're evidence of the mountain's distinctive quartzite bedrock. Mountain laurel adapts well by sinking its sinewy roots into the thin soil, and by doing so, this small understory tree with clusters of pink and white spring blossoms offers important erosion control.

At a particularly steep incline, a washout mars the hillside. Devoid of the stabilizing effects of the mountain laurel and other plants, the slope becomes a mini-chute that carries bucketloads of stone and dirt downhill after heavy rainstorms.

This washout and its related erosion is an apt metaphor for Sugarloaf as a whole. The mountain is a monadnock, a lump of resistant bedrock surrounded by relatively flat terrain. Textbooks say Sugarloaf's quartzite bedrock dates back 500 million years and the mountain formation itself resulted from the mountain-building activity of fourteen million years ago that created the Blue Ridge and the mountains to the north in Catoctin Mountain Park. To oversimplify, Sugarloaf's present condition is the culmination of fourteen million years of erosion.

Larger examples of the bedrock quartzite is on ample display on Sugarloaf's peak, where boulders and outcrops crown the top of the mountain. You can scramble atop them to catch views that span south and west across central Maryland farmland. The Potomac River is visible to the south, and South Mountain, which is part of the Blue Ridge chain of mountains, is the long dark ridge on the western horizon. Closer in, the summertime canopy of green-leafed oak and hickory trees far below beckon you to explore the preserve's trails.

The story of Sugarloaf is typical for Maryland's Piedmont region. In prehistoric times, Indians camped around the base of the mountain. At one time, the mountain was owned by the brother of a Maryland governor, and it was clear-cut for a charcoal-making operation. As the highest point for miles, its peak was used as a lookout during the Civil War. Confederate scouts watched Union forces cross the Potomac in 1864 en route to the Battle of Monocacy. Union forces occupied the same perch as a scouting point as control of the mountain traded sides throughout the war.

Early Maryland settlers saw in this mountain's distinctive profile a resemblance to their tall conical-shaped mounds of sugar—also known as sugarloafs.

View of Sugarloaf Mountain JENNIFER REED

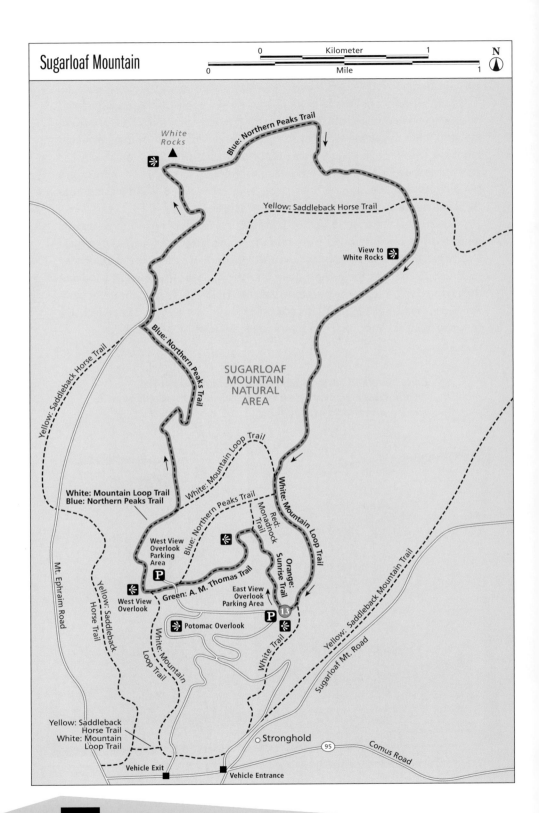

Kilometer

Mile

N

White Rocks

Blue: Northern Peaks Trail

Yellow: Saddleback Horse Trail

View to White Rocks

Yellow: Saddleback Horse Trail

Blue: Northern Peaks Trail

SUGARLOAF MOUNTAIN NATURAL AREA

White: Mountain Loop Trail

White: Mountain Loop Trail

White: Mountain Loop Trail Blue: Northern Peaks Trail

Blue: Northern Peaks Trail

Red: Monadnock Trail

West View Overlook Parking Area

Orange: Sunrise Trail

West View Overlook

Green: A. M. Thomas Trail

East View Overlook Parking Area

13

Mt. Ephraim Road

Yellow: Saddleback Horse Trail

White: Mountain Loop Trail

Potomac Overlook

Yellow: Saddleback Mountain Trail

White Trail

Sugarloaf Mt. Road

Yellow: Saddleback Horse Trail White: Mountain Loop Trail

Stronghold

95

Comus Road

Vehicle Exit

Vehicle Entrance

KID APPEAL

The short climb to the peak from East View or West View Overlook parking areas offers huge rewards for young children who can't handle longer climbs. Exercise caution with children along the rock outcrops that fringe the peak.

In the twentieth century, Sugarloaf's narrative took a twist. Gordon Strong, a wealthy industrialist, found the views here so spectacular that he bought the mountain and land around it. In 1946, he created the private nonprofit group Stronghold, Inc., that to this day continues to own, protect, and promote the preserve. Local history tells the story of how President Franklin Delano Roosevelt developed an intense interest in Sugarloaf as a site for a presidential retreat. Strong, a card-carrying Republican, resisted the offers and instead pointed Roosevelt north to mountainous country around Thurmont, Maryland. Thus, the official presidential retreat at Camp David is located in the Catoctin Mountains, not Sugarloaf.

As a result of Strong's ownership, Sugarloaf is today a unique amalgamation of developed property and preserved woodlands. There are carved stone steps built by the park's first superintendent, Albert M. Thomas. Winding paved roads lead almost to the summit, and there are traffic circles and lookouts with benches. The man-made landscaping blends in well with more than 3,000 acres of untouched woodland. In summertime, you can enjoy vistas from popular West View Overlook and within the hour stand atop White Rocks and feel as if you're the last person left on earth.

MILES AND DIRECTIONS

0.0 START from a trailboard sign at the East View Overlook parking area. Follow orange-blazed Sunrise Trail north as it climbs steeply through an understory of mountain laurel and blueberries. The path is wide and dirt. (**Note:** The unblazed dirt footpath that leads east from this trail junction leads to White Trail and is the return portion of this hike.)

0.3 Turn left (west) on red-blazed Monadnock Trail. (**FYI:** The term *monadnock* is a technical description of the geologic formation that is Sugarloaf Mountain.)

0.4 Reach the 1,282-foot summit of Sugarloaf Mountain. Views span west to the Potomac River and northwest to South Mountain and Catoctin. Turn left (south) on the green-blazed A. M. Thomas Trail.

0.5 Descend a long stone staircase and continue hiking downhill.

0.7 Reach the West View Overlook parking area. Stay left of a picnic pavilion and follow a stone path to an ornate stone staircase. Descend to a traffic circle with picnic tables in the middle. Turn right, begin to walk around the traffic circle counterclockwise, and locate a blue blaze on a chestnut oak. Enter the woods on the Northern Peaks Trail, a wide dirt footpath. (**FYI:** West View Overlook, a National Historic Landmark, is just to the left of this trailhead and is a worthy detour.)

0.8 Turn right (north) at a T junction where white-blazed Mountain Loop Trail merges with blue-blazed Northern Peaks Trail.

1.2 Turn left (north) and follow the blue-blazed Northern Peaks Trail. (**Bailout:** If you're pressed for time, follow the Mountain Loop Trail straight from this junction and return to East View Overlook in 2.5 miles. Resume below at mile 5.3.)

2.0 Exit the woods onto a paved road. Turn right (north), walk 300 feet downhill, and turn left to follow the road, which makes a hard left turn here. (**Note:** The Saddleback Horse Trail goes straight [north] from this hard left turn.)

2.1 Turn right (north) off the road and reenter the woods on a dirt path to begin a gradual climb.

2.9 Turn left (north) onto a spur trail to White Rocks. After enjoying the views, return to and turn left onto the Northern Peaks Trail. In quick succession, you will climb to two knobs in the ridgeline and pass through a clearing that boasts a 10-foot-high rock cairn.

White Rocks Flora and Fauna

White Rocks is one of four mountain knobs linked by the Northern Peaks Trail, a hikers-only path that leads away from West View Overlook parking area. As you traverse the western slope of Sugarloaf, the sound of cars drifts away. Where the route turns and begins its gradual descent to cross Mount Ephraim Road, there's a chance another jarring sound will fill your ears: the drum of a pileated woodpecker declaring its territory. Off the trailside, the broad leaves of false Solomon's seal serve as a reminder that this wildflower is part of the lily family. Its name is an unfortunate label—using the word *false* for what is truly a beautiful spring wildflower, with clusters of delicate white blossoms that remind you of a bursting star frozen in place. True Solomon's seal has demonstrated medicinal uses; its starchy root was used to treat ailments ranging from stomachaches to poor complexion. The so-called false variety, on the other hand, was better known as a source of food; its roots were cooked like asparagus.

4.0 Cross straight over the yellow-blazed Saddleback Horse Trail and reenter the woods on a single-track woods path.

4.4 After a short climb, top out onto the third knob in this ridgeline walk. Views span back north to White Rocks.

5.3 Turn left (south) and merge with the white-blazed Mountain Loop Trail. The trail for the next 0.1 mile is combined Mountain Loop Trail/Northern Peaks Trail. (**Note:** If you chose to shorten this circuit by following the Mountain Loop Trail where it split away from the Northern Peaks Trail [mile 1.2 above], resume directions from this point.)

5.4 Veer left (south) to remain on white-blazed Mountain Loop Trail. (**Note:** Blue-blazed Northern Peaks Trail forks right (west) to return to West View Overlook parking area.)

5.8 Turn right on a spur trail that leads uphill at a gradual slope.

5.9 HIKE ENDS at the East View Overlook parking area.

HIKE INFORMATION

Local information: Conference and Visitors Bureau of Montgomery County, Rockville, MD; (240) 777-2060; www.cvbmontco.com
Tourism Council of Frederick County, 19 E. Church St., Frederick, MD; (301) 644-4047; www.fredericktourism.org

Local events/attractions: Sugarloaf Mountain Vineyard, 18125 Comus Road, Dickerson, MD; (301) 605-0130; www.smvwinery.com. Grape stomp in Oct.

Good eats: Bassett's Fine Food & Spirits, 19950 Fisher Ave., Poolesville, MD; (301) 972-7443
Hyattstown Deli & Restaurant, 25901 Frederick Road, Clarkesburg, MD; (301) 607-4596. This is closer to the I-270 exit.

Local outdoor stores: Hudson Trail Outfitters, 401 N. Frederick Ave., Gaithersburg, MD; (301) 948-2474; www.hudsontrail.com

Organizations: Maryland Native Plant Society, Silver Spring, MD; www.mdflora.org

Other resources: *Sugarloaf: The Mountain's History, Geology and Natural Lore* and *An Illustrated Guide to Eastern Woodland Wildflowers and Trees: 350 Plants Observed at Sugarloaf Mountain, Maryland*, both by Melanie Choukas-Bradley and illustrated by Tina Thieme Brown

Any number of ways exist to approach a hike in Arlington National Cemetery. Starting a hike at Theodore Roosevelt Island links a memorial to our great president/conservationist with memorials to other great Americans. The short stint on Mount Vernon Trail offers a view far removed from Washington's iconic skyline. Arlington National Cemetery, with its acres of tree-shaded lawn and rows of uniform white tombstones, is a refuge of calm and contemplation.

Start: From the Theodore Roosevelt Island parking area on the George Washington Memorial Parkway

Distance: 6.1-mile loop

Approximate hiking time: 3 hours

Difficulty: Easy due to graded paths and easy terrain

Seasons: Apr through Oct

Other trail users: Bikers and joggers on the Mount Vernon Trail

Handicapped accessibility: Roads and walking paths in the cemetery are all paved and handicapped accessible, as is the Mount Vernon Trail.

Canine compatibility: Leashed dogs permitted

Land status: National cemetery

Fees and permits: No entrance fees or permits are required. If you choose to start this hike at the cemetery, there is a parking fee.

Schedule: The cemetery is open daily 8:00 a.m. to 7:00 p.m., Apr through Sept and daily 8:00 a.m. to 5:00 p.m. Oct through Mar

Facilities: Restrooms, visitor center, bookstore, historic mansion

Maps: DeLorme *Virginia Atlas & Gazetteer:* Page 77 A5. USGS 7.5 minute series: *Washington West, DC, MD, VA.* See also the National Park Service–issued walking map available at the visitor center information desk.

Trail contacts: Arlington National Cemetery, Arlington, VA 22211; (703) 607-8000; www.arlington cemetery.org

Special considerations: Please show respect and decorum in this solemn place. Joggers and bicyclists are not permitted inside the cemetery.

Finding the trailhead:

Distance from Washington, D.C.: 3 miles

From I-395 (Virginia): Follow I-395 northbound, making sure that you avoid the HOV-3 lanes that exit left after exit 8C. As you approach exit 10A-B, move to the left lane of I-395 and take left-branching exit 10C/Memorial Bridge. (*Note:* This is the last exit before crossing the Potomac River to Washington, D.C.) Merge onto the George Washington Memorial Parkway northbound. In 1.2 miles, stay to the right to avoid US 50, which branches left to Arlington National Cemetery. In 2.1 miles from I-395, turn left into the Theodore Roosevelt Island parking area.

Public transportation: Arlington National Cemetery is a stop on the Metro's Blue Line. Exit the station onto Memorial Drive South and pick up *Miles and Directions* below at mile 1.2, starting at the cemetery's visitor center. See www.mata.com for station details and train schedules.

Trailhead GPS: Theodore Roosevelt Island: N38 53.733' / W77 04.004'; Arlington National Cemetery Visitors Center: N38 52.991' / W77 03.943'

THE HIKE

It is hard to imagine Arlington National Cemetery looking any different than it does today: acres of green lawn; rows of white headstones; spectacular monuments to our country's greatest figures, both civilian and military. But, in fact, the property started not as a national cemetery, but as a memorial to our first president, George Washington.

As you walk Memorial Drive toward the white marble Memorial Entrance, your eyesight is drawn to a Greek Revival–style home, complete with white arches, that stands atop a hill. This is Arlington House, built by Washington's adopted son, George Washington Parke Custis, between 1802 and 1818. He stocked the home with memorabilia to Washington. In the surrounding fields, he rotated crops. Visitors were welcome to tour the building and listen as Custis retold stories of his famous father figure. In this home he raised his daughter, Mary Anna Randolph Custis, who would grow up to marry Robert E. Lee, future general of the Confederate Army during the Civil War.

After Custis's death, Lee and his wife lived in the home. When Lee took command of the Confederate Army, the house was abandoned, and later it was seized by the U.S. government. Over a circuitous route that saw it become a freedman's village for former black slaves, then a national cemetery, Arlington House and Lee were reunited—at least symbolically—when Arlington House was named a national memorial to Lee.

Trail. A single redbud tree has sprouted up inside the stone ruins of the house; in spring, it is a striking image of pink blossoms framed by the dark brown and green of the weathered stone. Farther up Fern Hollow on the left is a concrete box set into the ground, described as a "spring box" for tapping and storing clean water that seeped from a natural spring.

Fiddlehead ferns and skunk cabbage line the seasonal stream in Fern Hollow, giving it a vibrant green color in spring before the leaves break on the trees. The understory is thick with American beech trees, their tan, papery leaves from the previous fall still clinging to branches, waiting for the quill-like buds to push them aside for a new season of growth. As you climb higher, a forest floor of dry leaves, mountain laurel, and exposed rock showing the milky white of quartz and gray of feldspar indicate a change. A dry Appalachian forest slope so far east is only one reason naturalists and biologists study Bull Run Mountains ecosystems.

Huge boulders of rough stone, the white quartzite outcrops at this literal high point (1,311 feet), offer wide views west across the farmlands of Fauquier County

Chapman Family Cemetery

and the Blue Ridge. It is a singular view—no where else in Virginia can you have a west view of the Blue Ridge from such heights.

The mood of the woodland shifts yet again in the upper reaches of Catletts Branch. You have the option of following Quarry Trail as it climbs the east, or right-hand, hillside stream bank. The largest of this preserve's cemeteries is located here, composed entirely of unmarked gravestones. Similar markers in Dawson's Cemetery on Dawson's Trail gives rise to the speculation that these were the graves of servants and slaves.

Bypassing Quarry Trail, opt for an unmarked but clearly etched path through the stream's bottomland forest. It is a short 0.5 mile one-way, but en route it passes a quaint "rest stop" comprised of stone benches arranged in a circle. Eventually, this meandering path climbs a short hillside to the ruins of yet another home, marking a good turnaround spot. (A few hundred feet past this ruin, the trail clearly enters private property, marked by visible homes and surveyor's tape on trees.)

It took enterprising folks to carve a living from resources this mountain provided, whether it was the fruits and nuts of the trees or stone from the ground. Hand-dug veins mark old quarry sites, none more visible or striking as the trenches marked and visible from Quarry Trail. Here, on August 28, 1862, Union and Confederate forces faced each other and, shooting point-blank, engaged in an intense skirmish.

MILES AND DIRECTIONS

0.0 START from the trailboard kiosk on Beverley Mill Drive. Climb the railroad embankment, cross the tracks, and descend onto Mountain Road. (**FYI:** Spring rains make Mountain Road a messy trek.)

0.1 Turn left (west) onto Fern Hollow Trail. Over the next 0.3 mile this evenly graded footpath passes the remains of a brick-lined ice cellar, the old mill,

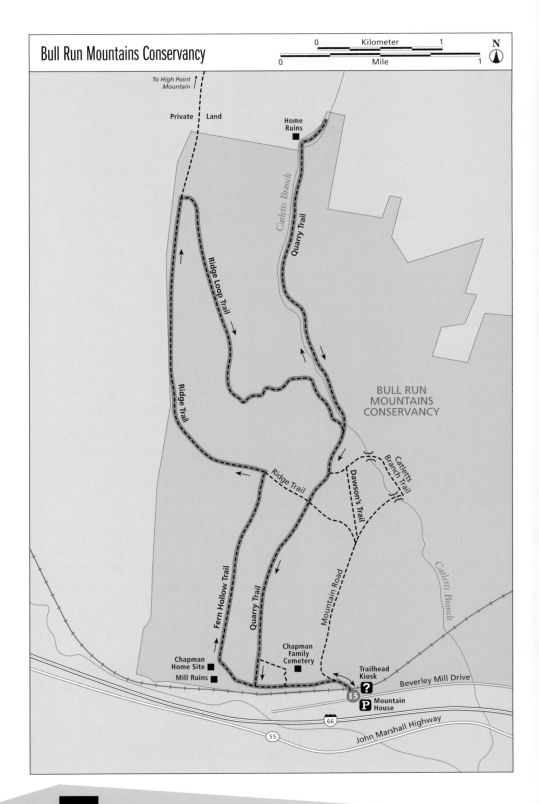

Bull Run Mountains Conservancy

and the Chapmans' eighteenth-century home site, plus side trails to Civil War battle trenches and the Chapman cemetery.

0.4 Ruins of a brick home and an old wooden mill mark Meadowlands, the Chapman family's home from the mid-1700s. Past this, swing right (north) on the black-blazed Fern Hollow Trail and climb a gentle uphill grade alongside a seasonal stream.

0.9 T junction with Ridge Trail. Turn left (west) onto the blue-blazed Ridge Trail and begin an uphill hike at a steeper grade, gaining 500 feet in slightly under 1 mile. Where the trail gains the ridgeline, there are several unmarked footpaths branching left to overlooks from Bull Run's west-facing quartzite cliffs.

1.8 Turn right (south) at a junction with the red-blazed Ridge Loop Trail. This trail descends gradually and then steeply down the dry, forested slopes of Bull Run Mountain. (**Note:** From the Ridge Loop Trail junction, an unmarked footpath leads 1.2 miles north to High Point Mountain, a series of rock outcrops at 1,311 feet with western views to the Blue Ridge Mountains. To make this trip, you must pass out of Conservancy-managed property. High Point Mountain is a private inholding. It is not public land, although the Blue Ridge Mountain Conservancy occasionally sponsors hikes to this area. Hikers are advised to check with staff at the Mountain house for a schedule of these hikes.)

2.5 Ridge Loop Trail ends at a junction with Quarry Trail. Turn left (north) on Quarry Trail, which is a wide dirt road. Immediately cross Catletts Branch and hike north through the lush bottomland forest.

3.1 Reach the ruins of old home foundations on a hillside overlooking the wide stream bottomland. Turn around and retrace your steps to the junction of Quarry Trail and Ridge Loop Trail.

3.7 At the junction of Quarry Trail and Ridge Loop Trail (mile 2.5 above), continue straight.

3.8 Reach a T junction with purple-blazed Catletts Branch Trail, which goes left (east). Continue straight (south) on Quarry Trail, which is a wide dirt road. (**Side trip:** Use Catletts Branch Trail, Mountain Road, and Dawson's Trail for a scenic 0.5-mile side trip. The highlight is a walk along Catletts Branch and

Before heading out on the trail, visit the student-made displays in the Mountain House. Check out the various kinds of rocks—granite, milky quartz—that you can pick up. Feel their weight and texture. Then try to identify them on the trail.

Dawson's Cemetery, where an ancient oak tree and scenic view of Catletts Branch make for a picturesque, contemplative spot.)

4.0   Cross Ridge Trail and continue straight (south) on Quarry Trail, which now becomes a footpath and climbs uphill.

4.5   Trenches on the right side of the trail mark the spot of a skirmish during the Battle of Thoroughfare Gap, August 28, 1862. From here, descend on Quarry Trail to a junction with Mill Trail.

4.6   Turn left (east) on Fern Hollow Trail.

4.7   Turn right (south) on Mountain Road.

4.8   HIKE ENDS at the trailboard kiosk on Beverley Mill Drive.

OPTIONS

Hikers looking for more miles and natural diversity can use Mountain Road to reach trails in the eastern region of the conservancy's holdings. East End Trail is the link between Mountain Road and LIttle Ridge Loop. See the Conservancy-issued map for more details.

HIKE INFORMATION

Local information: Prince William County/Manassas CVB, Manassas, VA; (703) 396-7130; www.visitpwc.com

Local events/attractions: Nearby, Manassas hosts festivals and historic-themed events throughout the year, including the annual Manassas Heritage Railway Festival in June, fireworks on the Fourth of July, and Civil War–related events throughout the year. For a complete schedule see www.visitpwc.com.

Good eats: Joe's Pizza & Subs, 14085 John Marshall Hwy., Gainesville, VA; (703) 754-2235. Great pizza and pasta dishes.

Local outdoor stores: REI, 11950 Grand Commons Ave., Fairfax, VA; (571) 522-6568; www.rei.com

Hudson Trail Outfitters, 9488 Fairfax Blvd., Fairfax, VA; (703) 591-2950; www.hudsontrail.com

Dick's Sporting Goods, Bull Run Plaza, 10800 Sudley Manor Dr., Manassas, VA; (703) 257-4300; www.dickssportinggoods.com

Hike tours: The Bull Run Mountains Conservancy conducts nature camps for children and monthly walks to explore old home sites and cemeteries, geology, amphibians, and more.

Great Falls Park

For generations, Great Falls was simply an obstacle to the flow of goods from western farms to eastern seaports. To walk along cliffs that line the river and delve into the Piedmont forest and study the ruins of the Patowmack Canal—predecessor to both the C&O Canal and New York's Erie Canal—is to capture a bit of the essence of a place both naturally and historically significant.

Start: From the park visitor center

Distance: 5.1-mile loop

Approximate hiking time: 2 to 3 hours

Difficulty: Easy because of well-traveled trails with a few short, steep sections along the river. The bushwhack from Difficult Run north to Ridge Trail, while not physically difficult, demands a hiker stay alert.

Trail surface: The trail from the park visitor center is graded and gravel lined. River Trail is uneven, crosses open rock, and has some pitchy stretches. Ridge Trail follows old dirt roads and forest paths. Swamp Trail is a unique, narrow dirt footpath alongside marsh.

Seasons: Springtime for the wildflowers and Oct for the foliage

Other trail users: Joggers, cross-country skiers, equestrians, mountain bikers, and rock climbers

Handicapped accessibility: Falls Overlooks 2 and 3 are fully accessible, as is the Patowmack Canal Trail to the Holding Basin

Canine compatibility: Leashed dogs permitted

Land status: National park

Fees and permits: Entrance fee (also valid for entry to Chesapeake & Ohio Canal National Historical Park in Maryland)

Schedule: Sunrise to sunset daily, except for Thanksgiving, Christmas, and New Year's Day

Facilities: Interpretive museum, theater, restrooms, snack bar (summer months only), picnic tables, visitor center

Maps: DeLorme *Virginia Atlas & Gazetteer:* Page 76 A3. USGS 7.5 minute series: *Vienna, VA* and *Falls Church, VA.*

Trail contacts: Great Falls Park, 9200 Old Dominion Drive, McLean, VA 22101; (703) 285-2965; www.nps.gov/grfa

Finding the trailhead:
Distance from Washington, D.C.: 17 miles
From I-495 (Capital Beltway): Take exit 13 and turn left onto Georgetown Pike/VA 193. Go 4.3 miles and turn right onto Old Dominion Drive to enter the park. From the park boundary drive 1.2 miles to the visitor center parking lot. Trailhead GPS: N38 59.820' / W77 15.277'

THE HIKE

More than 15 miles between Riverbend Park and Theodore Roosevelt Island, the Potomac River descends 130 feet. Technically, the river's passage spans the "fall line," a boundary between the Piedmont region of Virginia to tidewaters of the Coastal Plain. Such technicalities are washed away as you witness this transition from Overlooks 1 through 3 at Great Falls Park. The falls here are a roaring inferno of white water, an iconic image for most who visit the park.

After this grand watery tumult, the Potomac crams its daily average flow of 10,000 cubic feet per second into Mather Gorge. This mile-long chute averages a few hundred feet in width. Given that nearly 15,000 square miles of runoff drains into the Potomac from Virginia, Pennsylvania, and West Virginia, it comes as no surprise that during major storms, the 30- to 60-foot cliffs that form Mather Gorge on the Virginia side are washed over.

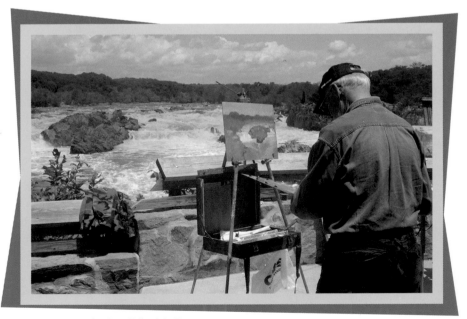

Painter captures the Great Falls of the Potomac

A section of River Trail traverses the cliff line of Mather Gorge. It's one of Great Falls Park's most popular foot routes. From the picnic area the pathway starts out wide and even, but soon it becomes winding and rocky underfoot. Dark gray angular rocks jut from the ground. This is stone—geologists call it schist and meta-graywacke—that supports the gorge bedrock. Short paths branch off River Trail, and on these you can either head to the high cliff line or descend into fissures that lead to the water's edge. Rock climbers, view seekers, and fishermen keep the trails well worn.

The advantage a hiker enjoys—especially one without an agenda, set path, or time frame—is that small things start to occupy your attention. It might be the perfectly smooth round holes in the rocks. It takes a geologist's sense of time to comprehend that these were formed hundreds of millions of years ago, when the river flowed at this level, and the potholes, as they're termed, were scoured by whirling sand and rock caught in a whirlpool effect.

A tree that appears, at first glance, to grow from solid rock has, on closer examination, actually found a toehold in a crevice filled with dirt. Grass sprouts from a pebble-and-sandbar along the river's edge. A pattern emerges as River Trail follows the shoreline. Here a rash of wildflowers, there a few bushes, and there a tree.

The rock and riverside habitats of the Potomac Gorge are increasingly drawing the attention of botanists, who have described bedrock terraces featuring Virginia pine and low shrubs. Down at river level are rocky bars and shores featuring a mix of hardwoods, like green ash and black willow, and grasses, like big bluestem. Whether they're 60 feet above the water on a cliff ledge or at the river's edge, they share one thing: They depend on the periodic disruption that comes with the flooding of the river.

River Trail eventually tails away from the Potomac River. Ridge Trail, Swamp Trail, and a variety of interconnecting dirt roads create a network of more than 12 miles covering more than 800 acres of preserved land. On a holiday weekend, a ranger at the contact station will process 125 cars an hour. Most flock to the Falls Overlooks, but others delve into the woodlands to walk under tall, thick-trunked tulip poplars. Young kids swarm the ruins of the old Patowmack Canal. Those who venture farther will find an unmarked route between Ridge Trail and Difficult Run.

KID APPEAL

Check out the Falls Overlooks, then explore canal ruins in the vicinity of Matildaville. There are hands-on lessons to be learned (namely in how goods were shipped before FedEx and UPS). Trace the path of the canal from the holding basin past Locks 1 and 2, and end at an overlook of the Canal Cut, where three locks brought laden boats through a narrow passage in the solid cliff walls that form Mather Gorge.

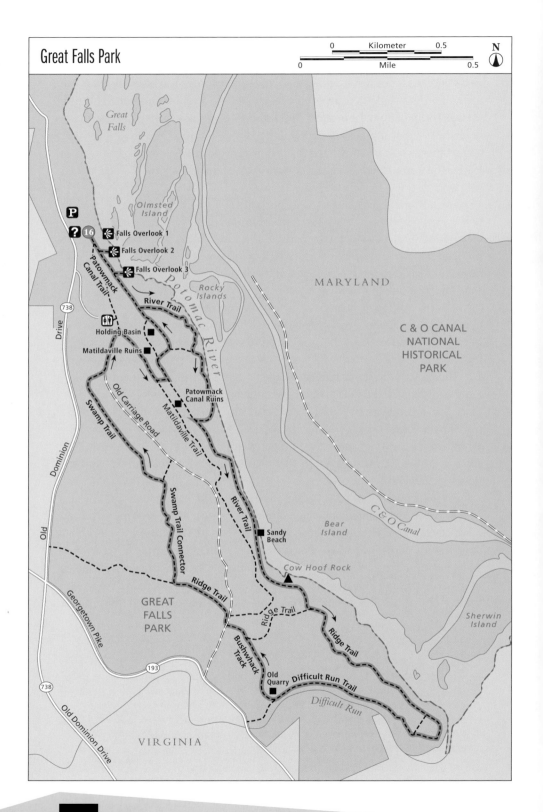

Great Falls Park

Kilometer
0   0.5

Mile
0   0.5

N

Great
Falls

Olmsted
Island

Falls Overlook 1

Falls Overlook 2

Falls Overlook 3

Patowmack Canal Trail

738

River Trail

Rocky
Islands

MARYLAND

Potomac River

Holding Basin

Matildaville Ruins

Old Carriage Road

Patowmack
Canal Ruins

C & O CANAL
NATIONAL
HISTORICAL
PARK

Swamp Trail

Matildaville Trail

River Trail

Sandy
Beach

Bear
Island

C & O Canal

Swamp Trail Connector

Dominion

Cow Hoof Rock

Old

Ridge Trail

GREAT
FALLS
PARK

Ridge Trail

Ridge Trail

Sherwin
Island

Georgetown Pike

738

193

Bushwhack Track

Old Quarry Difficult Run Trail

Difficult Run

Old Dominion Drive

VIRGINIA

On Swamp Trail, a low wetland positively pops with the green of skunk cabbage in springtime and remains lush all summer while the forest around it dries out.

And out on the cliff, a pine clings to its precarious perch, a reminder that the Potomac Gorge is, in the words of the Nature Conservancy, "one of the most important natural areas in the Eastern U.S."

MILES AND DIRECTIONS

0.0 START from the park visitor center. Walk around the building on a wide, graded path of dirt and crushed rock. Where the path splits, bear right (southeast). Once past the visitor center, turn left (east) onto the Falls Overlook Trail, which leads past Overlooks 1, 2, and 3.

0.2 Bear left (southeast) onto blue-blazed River Trail. The route starts out as a wide dirt path, and then narrows into a rocky footpath. (**Note:** The trail straight from this junction is the Patowmack Canal Trail and marks the return portion of this hike.)

0.5 Turn left (east) at a four-way trail intersection and descend a set of stairs to the edge of the Potomac. When you're finished exploring, return to this junction and turn left (east) to resume hiking the River Trail.

0.8 *Stay alert:* Turn right (west) on a dirt footpath for a detour around Canal Cut. Cross two boardwalks, and then turn left (south). Within 0.1 mile, the route returns to follow the cliffs high above Mather Gorge.

1.2 Cross straight over a paved service road and reenter woods opposite. Stay alert over the next 0.1 mile when River Trail runs close and parallel to the Matildaville Trail on the right.

1.4 Look for remains of a redbrick fireplace off the left side of the trail. A few hundred yards beyond this, look downhill to the left, where a sandy beach is visible. The trail here crosses exposed rock, and footing is tough and technical as you come to Cow Hoof Rock. (**FYI:** This promontory is your last chance to catch stellar views of the Potomac as it flows through Mather Gorge.)

1.6 A steep climb ends at a T junction with Ridge Trail. Turn left (south) onto Ridge, which is a wide dirt road.

2.1 Stay straight at a left turn in Ridge Trail. A footpath dives off the hillside to reach Difficult Run near its confluence with the Potomac. (**Note:** This short, steep descent is a bushwhack on an unmarked trail.). (**Option:** For a route that bypasses this bushwhack, turn right [west] just before 2.1 miles and follow the Ridge Trail downhill to Difficult Run, then turn right [north]. Resume mileage cues at 2.3 miles.)

2.2 Emerge from the wooded hillside onto Difficult Run Trail, a wide road of hard-packed dirt and gravel. Turn right (north) and walk along the stream. (**FYI:** Numerous side trails off to your left lead to overlooks onto Difficult Run and its many cascading falls.)

2.3 Stay straight (north) as the Ridge Trail intersects Difficult Run Trail from the right. (**Note:** If you opted for a right turn at 2.1 miles, resume mileage cues here.)

2.8 *Stay alert:* Turn right (north) on an unmarked footpath that climbs steeply uphill. (**Note:** This is a bushwhack on an established, but unmarked, trail. There are no trail signs or blazes at this junction. Prior to reaching it, look for a clearing on the right side of the trail that has the appearance of an old quarry—or a severely eroded hillside. If you reach Georgetown Pike, you've gone too far. Turn and retrace your steps.)

3.0 Veer left (north) onto Ridge Trail and descend in 0.1 mile to a junction with Old Carriage Road. Cross straight over the road and climb.

3.2 Turn right (north) onto the Swamp Trail Connector.

3.5 Turn left (northwest) onto Swamp Trail. (**Note:** This junction may not be marked, and the trail straight ahead [leading to Old Carriage Road] seems like the more obvious route. Swamp Trail is a single-track woodland path, while the spur is a wide, grassy path elevated above the low, wet ground on a berm.)

3.9 Turn left (north) onto Old Carriage Road.

4.1 Turn right (south) onto Matildaville Trail. (**FYI:** There is a bathroom a few feet north of this junction.)

4.3 Veer left and downhill where Matildaville Trail branches right and enters the woods as a narrow footpath. Descend to a T junction with Patowmack Canal Trail. Turn right and follow the old canal route to Lock 1. After exploring the ruins, return to this junction and continue straight (north) on the Patowmack Canal Trail. Look for side trails on the left that lead to ruins of the canal superintendent's home and other Matildaville homes.

4.6 Turn right at a fork in Patowmack Trail and cross the canal's holding basin. Within a few feet, a footbridge spans a small creek that was dug to control water levels in the holding basin. Beyond this footbridge, continue straight past a trail on the right that descends on a set of stairs to the River Trail.

4.7 Stay straight as a leg of the Patowmack Canal Trail merges on the left.

5.1 HIKE ENDS at the visitor center.

HIKE INFORMATION

Local information: Fairfax County/Capital Region Visitors Center, Tysons Corner Shopping Center, 2nd level, McLean, VA; (703) 752-9500; www.fxva.com

Local events/attractions: Wolf Trap National Park for the Performing Arts, Vienna, VA; (703) 255-1900; www.wolftrap.org

Good eats: Deli Italiano Gourmet Pizza & Subs, 762-B Walker Rd., Great Falls, VA; (703) 759-6782

The Old Brogue, 762-C Walker Rd., Great Falls, VA; (703) 759-3309

Local outdoor stores: Hudson Trail Outfitters, 9488 Fairfax Blvd., Fairfax, VA; (703) 591-2950; www.hudsontrail.com

REI, 11950 Grand Commons Ave., Fairfax, VA; (571) 522-6568; www.rei.com

Dick's Sporting Goods, Fair Lakes, 12501 Fair Lakes Circle, Fairfax, VA; (703) 803-0300; www.dickssportinggoods.com

Hike tours: Ranger-led programs and tours on nature and history are given throughout the year. The Sierra Club Potomac Region Outings (PRO) (202-547-2326; www.sierrapotomac.org) sponsors hikes throughout the region, including Great Falls Park. Participants do not need to be Sierra Club members.

Organizations: Friends of Great Falls, (301) 320-5035; www.friendsofgreatfalls .com

Washington, D.C., Chapter of the Sierra Club, (202) 363-4366; www.dc.sierraclub .org/contact/

Other resources: Learn more about Virginia's natural communities through Virginia's Department of Natural Heritage, www.dcr.virginia.gov/natural_heritage/

The historic Patowmack Canal

G. Richard Thompson Wildlife Management Area

The 4,000-acre area rises in a series of steep inclines to the crest of the Blue Ridge, with elevations ranging from 700 to 2,200 feet. The scenery is diverse, from fruit orchards surrounding old homesites to a serene trout pond to rocky outcrops. The network of trails includes a 7-mile section of the Appalachian Trail. There is an abundance of wildflowers—the area harbors one of the largest populations of large-flowered trillium in North America. Virginia's Native Plant Society lists the area on its register of important native plant sites.

Start: From parking area 7

Distance: 4.3-mile lollipop

Approximate hiking time: 2 hours

Difficulty: Easy

Trail surface: Dirt road, forest path

Seasons: In spring, when the large-flowered trillium are in bloom. Avoid the height of deer-hunting season, Nov through Jan.

Other trail users: Anglers, cyclists, equestrians, hunters (in season), and naturalists

Handicapped accessibility: Handicapped parking at the lake

Canine compatibility: Dogs must be leashed at all times outside of open hunting, chase, or training seasons.

Land status: State wildlife management area

Fees and permits: No fees. Appropriate hunting and fishing licenses are required. A trout license is required in addition to a Virginia fishing license.

Schedule: Dawn to dusk, daily, year-round.

Facilities: None

Maps: DeLorme *Virginia Atlas & Gazetteer:* Page 75 A5. USGS 7.5 minute series: *Linden, VA; Upperville, VA*

Trail contacts: Region 5 Office, Virginia Department of Game & Inland Fisheries, Fredericksburg, VA;, (540) 899-4169; www.dgif .virginia.gov/wmas

Other: Swimming in Thompson Lake is prohibited, however, anglers, hunters, and trappers lawfully engaged in those activities may wade in the lake. Primitive camping (no facilities) is allowed for up to 14 consecutive days.

Special considerations: Avoid the height of deer-hunting season, Nov through Jan

Finding the trailhead:
Distance from Washington D.C.: 71.5 miles
From I-66: Take exit 13; turn left and drive 0.2 mile south on VA 79. Turn left (east) onto VA 55 and drive 1.3 miles to Linden. Turn left (north) on Freezeland Road (VA 638). Drive 6 miles to where the road turns to gravel and becomes Fire Trail Road. Continue 0.1 mile to Parking Area 7 on the right. Trailhead GPS: N38 57.784' / W78 01.184'

THE HIKE

V irginia's Department of Game & Inland Fisheries oversees thirty wildlife management areas around the state with the hunter and angler in mind. Fields are kept clear to attract grazing animals, and seed plots are sown to keep them plump and healthy. Streams and man-made lakes are stocked with trout and other fish. As the state makes these areas hiker-friendly as well, they'd do well to model the G. Richard Thompson Wildlife Management Area in Fauquier County, where hikers and naturalists stake as much claim to the beautiful surroundings as outdoorsmen.

Canada geese on Thompson Lake

are plenty of distractions en route. You may see a snake crossing the path or even a box turtle. Left unmolested, this reptile could live more than sixty years. To tell its age, look at the shell. If it's 5 inches or smaller the turtle is probably ten years old or younger.

MILES AND DIRECTIONS

0.0   START from parking area 7. Hike down the chained-off road that drops off the left side of the parking lot. The road is gravel at first, then reverts to dirt and grass.

0.2   Walk straight past a junction with the Appalachian Trail (AT) on the Lake Trail. (**Side trip:** A right on the AT leads to Manassas Gap Shelter in 3 miles.)

0.5   A grass road veers off on the right. Continue straight downhill on the main grass road.

0.6   Continue straight downhill past another grass road that turns right into a clearing.

1.3   The trail levels, and on both sides, remnants of stone walls are visible. Make note of the overgrown, unblazed Stone Wall Trail branching off to the left. You'll return to it later. Curve to the right (south).

1.8   The road emerges from the cover of trees. Ahead is a nice view across a valley to a farm on the opposite hill.

1.95   Reach Lake Thompson. Retrace your steps back to Stone Wall Trail.

2.6   At the intersection with the Lake Trail, turn right onto Stone Wall Trail, crossing an old stone wall.

2.9   Pass by some large boulders in the woods to the left and climb steeply.

3.0   Emerge from the woods onto the AT. Continue walking straight ahead on the singletrack, white-blazed trail. (**Side trip:** The AT downhill to the right reaches Dick's Dome Shelter in 0.3 mile.)

4.1   The AT emerges onto a grass road. Turn right onto the Lake Trail and head uphill.

4.3   HIKE ENDS at Parking Area 7.

Who was George Richard Thompson? He was an avid hunter who bequeathed the land to the state for the enjoyment of future hunters.

OPTIONS

The 2-mile Ted Lake Loop begins at Parking Area 4 and includes many interesting features including a trillium field, some homesite ruins, and the Manassas Gap AT Shelter.

HIKE INFORMATION

Local Information: Warrenton-Fauquier County Visitor Center, 205-1 Keith Street, P.O. Box 127, Warrenton, VA 20188; (540) 347-4414; www.fauquierchamber.org

Local Events/Attractions: Linden Vineyards, 3708 Harrels Corner Road, Linden; (540) 364-1997; www.lindenvineyards.com

Good Eats: Hunter's Head Tavern, 9048 John Mosby Hwy. (U.S. 50), Upperville; 540-592-9020; www.huntersheadtavern.com. English-themed pub in a 1750 log cabin with Guinness on tap, fish and chips, and a hearty, crusty bread. The pub menu is half-price from 3 to 6 p.m.

Local Outdoor Store: Mountain Trails, 212 East Cork St., Winchester; (540) 667-0030; www.mountain-trails.com

Hike Tours: The Piedmont Chapter of the Virginia Native Plant Society, P.O. Box 336, The Plains, VA 20198; (540) 837-1600; www.vnps.org. Leads trillium walks in May and invasive species removal days.

Organizations: Potomac Appalachian Trail Club (PATC), 118 Park Street SE, Vienna, VA 22180-4609; (703) 242-0693; www.patc.net

---

KID APPEAL

The 10-acre Lake Thompson is stocked with trout, is frequented by ducks and geese, and is a pleasant, green space to have a picnic.

This "quadruple crown" of hikes touches on four high points in three different states: Split Rock in Virginia, Maryland Heights and Stone Fort in Maryland, and Jefferson Rocks in West Virginia. Front and center at each is the Potomac River and the picturesque town of Harpers Ferry, West Virginia, perched on a point at the confluence of the Shenandoah and Potomac Rivers. The Appalachian Trail weaves them together for a full day of climbing and a dash of history.

Start: From River Access parking area on Shenandoah St.

Distance: 12.1-mile loop

Approximate hiking time: 4 to 5 hours

Difficulty: Difficult due to the distance, several steep climbs, and the proximity to highways and traffic

Trail surface: The Appalachian Trail utilizes woodland footpaths, sidewalks, footbridges, town streets, and stone steps. The C&O Canal towpath is a level, graded dirt path. Old dirt roads and forest paths characterize trails through Maryland Heights.

Seasons: Best in all seasons

Other trail users: Joggers and mountain bikers on paved sections; motorists on roadways

Handicapped accessibility: The *Accessible Route Map for Lower Town* is available at the visitor center, by calling the visitor center, or online at www.nps.gov/hafe/planyourvisit/maps.htm

Canine compatibility: Leashed dogs permitted

Land status: National historical park

Fees and permits: Entrance fee

Schedule: Park is open daily 8:00 a.m. to 5:00 p.m.; closed Thanksgiving, Christmas, and New Year's Day

Facilities: Restrooms, picnic tables, visitor center, bookstore, historic buildings

Maps: DeLorme *West Virginia Atlas & Gazetteer:* Page 31 H7. USGS 7.5 minute series: *Harpers Ferry, WV, VA, MD.* PATC Map 7, AT in Northern Virginia (Potomac River to VA 7). The information desk at Harpers Ferry National Historic Park supplies line-drawn trail maps.

Trail contacts: Harpers Ferry National Historical Park, P.O. Box 65, Harpers Ferry, WV 25425; (304) 535-6029; www.nps.gov/hafe Potomac Appalachian Trail Club (PATC), 118 Park St. SE, Vienna, VA 22210; (703) 242-0314; www .potomacappalachian.org
Other: This route passes two convenience stores: Tri-State Exxon, at US 340 and VA 617, and the Sandy

Hook Grocery, just west of the US 340 bridge on Sandy Hook Road
Special considerations: Sections of this route involve hiking alongside busy US 340 and crossing an active railroad line. Use extra caution on a 0.4-mile section of this route along the US 340 road shoulder from the Loudoun Heights Trail to the Potomac River.

Finding the trailhead:

Distance from Washington, D.C.: 65 miles

From Frederick, MD: From the junction of I-70 and US 340/15, take US 340/15 south. In 4 miles, continue on US 340 as US 15 splits south to Virginia. In another 12 miles, cross the Potomac River into Virginia. Follow US 340 as it crosses the Shenandoah River into West Virginia. Immediately turn right onto Shenandoah Street. Within 0.1 mile, turn right into the River Access parking area.

From Leesburg, VA: Take US 15 north from its junction with VA 7. In 12.4 miles, cross the Potomac River into Maryland. Continue north on US 15 and, in 7 miles, merge onto US 340 south. In 11.5 miles from this merge, cross the Potomac River into Virginia. In another 2 miles, cross the Shenandoah River into West Virginia. Immediately, turn right onto Shenandoah Street. Within 0.1 mile, turn right into the River Access parking area. Trailhead GPS: N39 19.302'/ W77 44.581'

THE HIKE

The advantage height offers is clear from the rocky promontory called Maryland Heights. The unobstructed view drops to the Potomac and Shenandoah Rivers and across to the small town of Harpers Ferry, West Virginia. "So long as Maryland Heights was occupied by the enemy, Harpers Ferry could never be occupied by us," wrote Maj. Gen. Lafayette McLaws of the Confederate Army.

Confederates won the battle by occupying three high points surrounding the town: Maryland Heights, Loudoun Heights, and Bolivar Heights. Captured were 12,500 Union troops, which is described as the largest single capture of Federal troops during the Civil War. With the exception of Bolivar Heights, these vistas are connected by a network of trails and roads. To reach these, and Jefferson Rock

Leesylvania State Park

Leesylvania State Park's trails are short, easy to hike, and fun. You'll find a virtual textbook worth of American history along the Lee's Woods Historic Trail. The bluff on Freestone Point was the site of a Civil War artillery. Colonial-era farmers rolled hogsheads of tobacco down to the water's edge for loading and shipment to England. Even up through the 1950s speculators looked to cash in on the beautiful Potomac waterfront with proposals for gambling boats and theme parks. There is a quiet side to the park as well, a place along Powell's Creek Nature Trail where you can learn the natural story of a small Potomac River tributary.

Start: Lee's Woods Historic Trail: From a trailboard sign and map near the Freestone Point Fishing Pier. Powell's Creek Nature Trail: From a trailboard sign and map in the Powell's Creek Nature Trail parking area.

Distance: Lee's Woods, 1.7-mile loop; Powell's Creek: 1.6-mile loop

Approximate hiking time: 1 hour for each loop

Difficulty: Easy due to level, graded paths; minimum elevation gain; and well-marked routes

Trail surface: Gravel and dirt paths, gravel and dirt roads, forested trail, stairs

Seasons: Best in late fall, winter, and early spring when the crowds thin out and bare trees allow for better views of the water

Other trail users: Hikers and joggers only

Handicapped accessibility: The 1-mile Bushy Point Trail and the Potomac Trail through the picnic area and along the waterfront

Canine compatibility: Leashed

dogs permitted

Land status: State park

Fees and permits: Per-vehicle entrance fee

Schedule: Dawn to dusk daily

Facilities: Restrooms, picnic shelters, visitor center, campground, camp store, boat ramp, marina

Maps: DeLorme *Virginia Atlas & Gazetteer:* Page 76 D4. USGS 7.5 minute series: *Quantico, VA, MD.* Line-drawn maps are available from the state park visitor center or ranger contact station at the park entrance.

Trail contacts: Leesylvania State Park, 2001 Daniel K. Ludwig Dr., Woodbridge, VA 22191; (703) 730-8205; www.dcr.virginia.gov/ state_parks/lee.shtml

Finding the trailhead:
Distance from Washington, D.C.: 29 miles
From I-95: Take exit 156 (Dale City/Rippon Landing) and follow signs for VA 784 eastbound. After driving 0.9 mile on VA 784, merge right onto US 1 South. Drive another 0.9 mile to Neabsco Hill Road, where you turn left onto Neabsco and drive 1.5 miles to Daniel K. Ludwig Drive. Turn right onto Ludwig Drive and in 2.2 miles reach the ranger contact station. Trailhead GPS: Lee's Woods Historic Trail: N38 35.454' / W77 14.876'; Powell's Creek Nature Trail: N38 35.567' / W77 15.680'

THE HIKE

A sharp scent of low tide drifts landward and over Freestone Point. Wind ruffles leaves on the small trees that cover the slope. It's 110 feet down to the sandy water's edge of Occoquan Bay. Atop this sandy bluff, the ground is pockmarked with sunken pits and earthen mounds. It was here that Confederate soldiers under the orders of Gen. Robert E. Lee placed cannon here to fire on Union gunships sailing up the Potomac toward Washington, D.C.

Lee knew of Freestone Point's strategic value firsthand. It and the land around it were his family's ancestral lands. It was his great-grandfather's home site and the birthplace of his father, Revolutionary War hero Light Horse Harry Lee. Its military value lay in its broad view of the Potomac. The Confederacy had no navy to speak of, but they could—and did—harass Union navy sailing the Potomac to and from Washington, D.C. Freestone Point was one of several gun placements on Potomac bluffs stretching south to Chopawamsic Creek. In the fall of 1861, Union sloops fired on the position, and Confederate soldiers returned fire. It was the height of activity for this battery as the theater of war moved farther inland.

Brief as it was, this interlude with a Civil War moment is telling of Leesylvania State Park as a whole, and the 1.7-mile Lee's Woods Historic Trail in particular. Here, it is the breadth of history, not size or pristine condition, that characterizes the park. Where another park's value may lie in its old-growth forest or rare plants, Leesylvania offers hikers a chance to tap into almost every era of American history up to, and including, the Great Depression of the 1920s and 1930s.

"At the point of rock" is the translation of the American Indian word neabsco. It describes the high bluff of land more commonly known as Freestone Point. The location of Freestone Point is indicated on maps from the eighteenth century and was an important landmark for river pilots when navigating the Potomac.

0.8 Enter a clearing and turn right (north) on a woods path that leads to the ancestral home of the Lee family. A spur trail leads left (west) from this clearing to a family cemetery.

1.0 Reach the Lee and Fairfax family cemetery, surrounded by a wrought-iron fence. (**Side trip:** Behind the cemetery, follow the red-blazed footpath left into the woods for fifty steps to an observation point overlooking a historic railroad gap. Past here, the trail covers a short, but pitchy, route that ends on a knoll with stellar spring and winter views of Occoquan Bay. After exploring, return to the Lee and Fairfax cemetery and follow the red blazes east.)

1.2 Continue straight (east) on the Lee's Woods Historic Trail at a junction with a fire road on the right.

1.4 Emerge from the woods trail to views of the historic Fairfax home. Turn left and descend on a gravel road. Ahead, pass by the trail on the left that climbs to river overlooks and the Civil War battery.

1.7 HIKE ENDS at the Lee's Woods trailboard and sign.

Fairfax House ruins

19

> *Local students from the Freedom High School contributed the artistic renditions of plants and animals that decorate trailboards along Powell's Creek Nature Trail.*

Trail 2: Powell's Creek Nature Trail

0.0 START from a trailboard sign and map in the Powell's Creek Nature Trail parking area. Follow a rock-lined path into the woods behind the sign. Pass a newly constructed section of the Potomac Heritage National Scenic Trail that merges with Powell's Creek Nature trail on the right. Continue to follow blue blazes of the Powell's Creek trail.

0.2 Bear left (south) at another fork in the trail. (**Note:** The trail right from this junction is the return portion of this hike.)

0.5 Turn right (west) to continue on Powell's Creek Nature Trail at a junction with Bushy Point Trail. Descend steps dug into the dirt footpath, and then cross a seeping wetland on a footbridge. The trail arches left (west) to follow the stream. (**Note:** If you're following the route described under *Options*, turn left here to follow Bushy Point Trail and the Potomac Trail to Lee's Woods Historic Trail in 1.25 miles.)

0.6 Climb a set of stairs, and then turn left to reach an overlook onto Powell's Creek.

0.7 Veer left off the nature trail onto an unmarked path that descends to the river. Where it splits, veer left again.

0.8 Reach the bottom and a split rail fence. Take in the views of Powell's Creek and the railroad bridge, and then retrace your steps uphill. When you reach the nature trail, turn left (north) to continue the loop.

1.4 Bear left at a V junction with the first leg of the loop.

1.6 HIKE ENDS at the parking area.

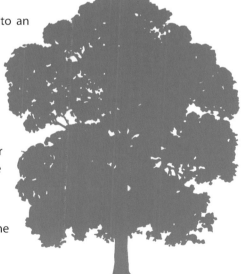

OPTIONS

You can connect the Powell's Creek Nature Trail and Lee's Woods Historic Trail by using the park's Potomac Trail and Bushy Point Trail. This option adds 1.25 miles and makes the hike an end-to-end trip requiring a shuttle. Also, a newly constructed segment of the Potomac Heritage National Scenic Trail connects Powell's Creek Nature Trail to Neabsco Hill Road.

HIKE INFORMATION

Local information: Prince William County Visitor Information Center, 200 Mill St., Occoquan, VA; (703) 491-4045; www.visitpwc.com

Local events/attractions: Monthly evening musical performances take place at the park's marina June through mid-Sept

Good eats: Tim's Rivershore Restaurant & Crabhouse, 1510 Cherryhill Rd., Dumfries, VA; (703) 441-1375; www.timsrivershore.com. Enjoy fresh seafood and views of the Potomac River.

Local outdoor stores: Modell's Sporting Goods, Potomac Mills, Woodbridge, VA; (703) 499-9696; www.modells.com

Hike tours: Park staff offer history and nature hikes and canoe trips

Organizations: Friends of Leesylvania State Park, Woodbridge, VA; (703) 583-6904

Prince William Conservation Alliance advocates for conservation of Prince William County's fast-disappearing woodlands. Their Web site, www.pwconserve .org, has a page dedicated to Powell's Creek.

Other resources: *A Potomac Legacy: Lee's Woods Historical Interpretive Trail* and *Powell's Creek Nature Trail*, booklets produced by the Department of Conservation & Recreation, are available in the park visitor center

> 🌿 **Green Tip:**
> *When you just have to go, dig a hole 6–8 inches deep and at least 200 feet from water, camps, and trails. Carry a zip-lock bag to carry out toilet paper, or use a natural substitute such as leaves instead (but not poison ivy!!!). Fill in the hole with soil and other natural materials when you're done.*

Manassas National Battlefield Park

The grasslands and forests of Manassas National Battlefield Park offer a bucolic setting for a day hike that is steeped in Civil War history. The Battle of First Manassas in the summer of 1862 was a victory for the South. Historians point to it as the first sign the War Between the States would be a longer, more protracted fight than many believed or hoped. The Battle of Second Manassas opened the door for the South's first invasion of the North. In places like Deep Cut, Chinn Ridge, and the Unfinished Railroad, this battlefield's rich history is as palpable as the fields and pastures, woods and wetlands are beautiful.

Start: From the park visitor center

Distance: 8.6-mile loop

Approximate hiking time: 4 hours

Difficulty: Moderate due to length, but with gently rolling terrain and only a few steep climbs

Trail surface: Dirt footpaths, gravel paths, mowed grass paths, old farm roads, and paved roads

Seasons: Spring and fall

Other trail users: Mountain bikers, horseback riders

Handicapped accessibility: At Chinn Ridge, number 9 on the battlefield driving tour, a 0.3-mile paved path leads past historic markers. The Second Manassas Battlefield driving tour is 16 miles and covers 11 sites of interest from both the First and Second Manassas battles.

Canine compatibility: Leashed dogs permitted

Land status: National battlefield park

Fees and permits: Entrance fee (good for three days' admission)

Schedule: Open dawn until dusk, 365 days a year. The visitor center is open daily 8:30 a.m. to 5:00 p.m. except Thanksgiving and Christmas.

Facilities: The visitor center features restrooms, interpretive displays, a soda machine, and a bookstore. There are picnic tables in a grove of trees adjacent to the parking area.

Maps: DeLorme *Virginia Atlas & Gazetteer:* Page 76 B1. USGS 7.5 minute series: *Gainesville, VA.* See also National Geographic's TOPO! software, Mid-Atlantic Region, Disc 4. The park visitor center provides free maps upon request. History buffs can follow this hiking route using *The Manassas Battlefields* map, part of Cleverish Map Co.'s Civil War Watercolor Map Series (available in the park service bookstore).

Trail contacts: Manassas National Battlefield Park, 12521 Lee Hwy., Manassas, VA 20109; (703) 361-1339; www.nps.gov/mana/contacts.htm

Other: Possession and/or use of metal detectors in the battlefield park is prohibited. Hikers should be on alert for ticks during summer months.

Finding the trailhead:

Distance from Washington, D.C.: 35 miles

From I-66: Take exit 47B for VA 234 North. Drive 0.7 mile north and turn right into Manassas National Battlefield Park, following signs for the visitor center. In 0.1 mile, park in the lot at the top of Henry Hill. Trailhead GPS: N38 48.776' / W77 31.290'

Hiking past replica cannon

THE HIKE

More so than the open fields that characterize much of Manassas National Battlefield Park, the Unfinished Railroad has an air of solemnity about it. This old earthen berm was built prior to the Civil War, intended to support a railroad between Manassas Gap Railroad and the port city of Alexandria.

During the Second Battle of Manassas, Gen. Thomas "Stonewall" Jackson used 2 miles of the railroad bed as his line of defense. Jackson had earned his nickname during the First Battle of Manassas in July 1861, when a fellow general is purported to have rallied his troops with the cry: "There is Jackson standing like a stone wall." Along with it, Jackson had a well-earned reputation as a brilliant military strategist. Selection of the Unfinished Railroad, a natural line of defense, was but one indicator of this.

The woodlands that surround the Unfinished Railroad heighten the atmosphere, which makes the scenery around Deep Cut all the more striking. Climbing from the woods to the top of the old railroad bed on a wooden staircase, a scene of widespread destruction unfolds for acres in every direction: Trees are uprooted. There are large piles of brush. Wide tractor and tire tracks mark where heavy equipment operated.

What one person may view as destructive, however, another may see as restorative. The Deep Cut Landscape Restoration project is an effort to restore 140 acres of battlefield land into grasslands. By doing so, the National Park Service accomplishes two goals: to restore this area as closely as possible to how it was during the Civil War (generations of farming and tree planting in the last 150 years have altered the battlefield) and restore native grasslands, a habitat type that is fast shrinking in Virginia. The park service estimates that the state has lost more than half of its grasslands since 1945. With it goes habitat for songbirds, owls, raptors, and small mammals like field mice.

MILES AND DIRECTIONS

0.0 START at the east end of the visitor center parking lot, at a sign that reads: FIRST MANASSAS TRAIL/HENRY HILL LOOP TRAIL. Follow the mowed path through an open field. Beyond a line of replica cannons, a blue-blazed trail stick marks where the meadow path enters the woods. (**FYI:** The cannons approximate where Confederate soldiers held a line of defense against an advancing Union Army during the First Battle of Manassas, July 21, 1861.)

0.6 Turn left (north) onto a wide, graded road, First Manassas Trail, lined with crushed rock. (**Note:** A horse trail parallels the hiking trail for the next 0.3 mile.)

3.0   Pass a spur trail on the left for the Carter Family Cemetery.

3.6   Continue straight past Matthews Hill Loop Trail on the left. In 0.2 mile, turn right (south) at a four-way junction and descend 0.1 mile to the Matthews Hill Loop parking lot. (**Bailout:** A left turn on the Matthews Hill Loop leads back to the park visitor center via the Stone House in 1.5 miles.)

3.9   Pass through the Matthews Hill Loop parking lot. As a handrail, use the historic marker for the New York national guard unit that drove Confederates off Matthews Hill during the Battle of First Manassas. Pass a trailhead for the red-blazed Stone House Trail, which leads south 1.2 miles to the park visitor center. Cross VA 234/Sudley Road, turn right (north), and follow a path lined with wood chips.

4.5   After tracing the edge of a field, turn right (west) as the Second Manassas Trail becomes a wide dirt lane shaded by cedar trees.

5.0   Enter the parking area for the Unfinished Railroad Loop Trail. Cross VA 622/Featherbed Lane and look for a sign that reads SECOND MANASSAS TRAIL / BRAWNER FARM 1.0 MILE. This trailhead is marked by fence stiles intended to block mountain bikes and horses. Climb a short set of stairs and enter the woods, heading southwest. (**Note:** Avoid the horse trail that heads west into the woods from this spot. It is the wider and more graded of the two

Handicapped trail along the Fight at the Fences

trails.) (**Side trip:** The Unfinished Railroad Loop is a worthwhile 1.1-mile trip along cuts and fills of what was, in the 1850s, intended as a railroad line linking the Manassas Gap Railroad with the port city of Alexandria. The earthen berms formed a natural line of defense used by Gen. Thomas J. "Stonewall" Jackson during the Second Battle of Manassas in 1862.)

5.3 Climb a set of wooden stairs to the top of the Unfinished Railroad embankment. Enter a cut-over area, the result of a park-sponsored habitat restoration project. (**FYI:** The Deep Cut / Brawner Farm habitat restoration project involves cutting down 140 acres of trees to restore the area to grassland habitat the park says more accurately reflects conditions at the time of the Civil War.)

5.5 Turn left (east) at a tall brick historic marker. Keep the marker on your right as you pick your way through tree and limb debris. Walk downhill on a mowed grass path to a small stream.

5.8 Cross VA 622/Featherbed Lane, turn right (south), and walk across a driveway apron of crushed rock, keeping on your left a metal gate that blocks the driveway. Walk south on an open path bordered by a split rail fence on your left and the road on your right.

6.3 Cross US 29/Lee Highway at a four-corners intersection. Walk south alongside VA 622/Featherbed Lane for about 100 feet, then veer left (southeast) to pass through a gap in the split rail fence. The trail is now a mowed grass path heading southeast through a wide meadow.

6.6 Enter a clearing with three large monuments dedicated to the New York 5th and 10th Regiments. Here, the trail is a dirt path that skirts the paved rotary. Reenter the woods, heading south at a blue-blazed trail stick. The trail through the woods is wide and graded, lined with crushed stone.

6.8 Cross Young's Branch on a wooden footbridge, then turn right (south), following blue-blazed trail sticks. (**Note:** The dirt trail that goes straight uphill from this junction is the return leg of the Chinn Ridge Loop Trail.)

7.6 Walk straight (north) past a trail on the left (the return leg of the Chinn Ridge Loop Trail). Keep a parking lot to your right as you follow a mowed grass path. Past the parking lot, the trail joins a paved path.

7.9 Turn right at a marker detailing the death of Fletcher Webster, son of famed American statesman Daniel Webster. Climb a small hill and look for a blue-blazed trail stick in the northwest corner of the clearing. (**Note:** Stay alert for this historic marker. There is no trail marker indicating the turn off the paved path.)

8.1 At a junction with a paved road, turn left (north) and walk along the road shoulder.

8.4 Cross VA 234/Sudley Road and climb the paved driveway for the park visitor center.

8.6 HIKE ENDS at the park visitor center.

HIKE INFORMATION

Local information: Historic Manassas, Inc., 9431 West St., Manassas, VA; (877) 848-3018; www.visitmanassas.org. The visitor center in Old Town Manassas is located in the restored 1914 train depot.

Local events/attractions: The Manassas Farmers' Market (703-361-6599; www.visitmanassas.org) takes place Thurs and Sat, Apr through mid-Nov, in Old Town. Get great local produce and baked goods.

Local outdoor stores: REI, 1950 Grand Commons Ave., Fairfax, VA; (571) 522-6568; www.rei.com

Dick's Sporting Goods, Bull Run Plaza, 10800 Sudly Manor Dr., Manassas, VA; (703) 257-4300; www.dickssportinggoods.com

Eastern Mountain Sports, 22000 Dulles Retail Plaza, Dulles, VA; (703) 421-4330; www.ems.com

Hudson Trail Outfitters, 9488 Fairfax Blvd., Fairfax, VA; (703) 591-2950; www.hudsontrail.com

Hike tours: The park service offers daily walking tours of the battlefield

Organizations: Friends of Manassas National Battlefield Park (Manassas, VA; www.fmnbp.org) partners with the Potomac Appalachian Trail Club (PATC) to help develop and maintain hiking and interpretive trails within the park

Other resources: National Park Civil War Series books: *The First Battle of Manassas* and *The Second Battle of Manassas*

Mason Neck State Park

Bordered by Mason Neck National Wildlife Refuge, Pohick Bay Regional Park, and Gunston Hall historic plantation, 1,813-acre Mason Neck State Park is part of 5,600 acres of remarkably undisturbed wildlife habitat on this peninsula just minutes from Northern Virginia's urban sprawl. Gazing on views like these, George Mason framed the Virginia Declaration of Rights at his nearby home. Listen to the sounds of the marsh and forest, and reflect on the blue expanse of Belmont Bay. When you're done hiking the trails, you can head to the adjacent refuge, created to protect vital habitat for nesting bald eagles.

Start: From the visitor center

Distance: 5.6-mile loop

Approximate hiking time: 3 hours

Difficulty: Easy due to its short length, level terrain, and wide, well-marked, and graded trails

Trail surface: Gravel, stairs, boardwalk, forested trail, footbridge, paved road

Seasons: Best in winter, when both resident and migrant bald eagle activity is high

Other trail users: Hikers only, except for the paved High Point Multi-Use Trail, which can accommodate joggers, strollers, wheelchairs, and bikes

Handicapped accessibility: High Point Multi-Use Trail is paved, as is the 300-yard paved trail to an observation platform on Belmont Bay. Dogue Trail is gravel.

Canine compatibility: Leashed dogs permitted

Land status: State park

Fees and permits: Per-vehicle entrance fee

Schedule: Open daily 8:00 a.m. to dusk (gate locked at 8:00 p.m.)

Facilities: Restrooms, visitor center, camping, environmental center, boat ramp, playground, campground. There is spigot for fresh water behind the visitor center.

Maps: DeLorme *Virginia Atlas & Gazetteer:* Page 77 C4. USGS 7.5 minute series: *Ft. Belvoir, VA, MD.* A hand-drawn map is available at the nature center.

Trail contacts: Mason Neck State Park, 7301 High Point Rd., Lorton, VA 22079; (703) 339-2385; www.dcr.virginia.gov/state_parks/mas.shtml

Special considerations: Swimming is not allowed from the park shoreline

Finding the trailhead:
Distance from Washington, D.C.: 26 miles
From I-95: Take exit 163 for Lorton/VA 642. Turn left onto VA 642 East and drive 0.8 mile to Armistead Road. Turn right onto Armistead, following signs for Pohick Bay Regional Park and Gunston Hall. In 0.2 mile, turn right onto US 1 South (also called Richmond Highway). In 0.8 mile, turn left onto VA 242/Gunston Road. (*Note:* After passing Pohick Bay Regional Park, Gunston Road becomes VA 600.) In 4.5 miles, Gunston Road forks. Here, bear right onto High Point Road, following the sign for Mason Neck State Park and Mason Neck Wildlife Refuge. In 0.8 mile, enter the state park. The ranger station is 0.2 mile from the park boundary, and the visitor center is 1.7 miles from the park boundary. Trailhead GPS: N38 38.644' / W77 11.947'

THE HIKE

With every footstep along the Bay View Trail, nature springs into action. A turtle pokes its head above water; frogs sense our approach and hit the water with a *kerplunk*. A log rolls slightly as a painted turtle cuts short its sunning and slips into the water. Then the sight that freezes us in our tracks: A writhing conga line of tent caterpillars stretching along the boardwalk for 10 feet or so.

The first reaction—"Gross!"—lasts a minute or two, but the longer we watch, the more this parade fascinates. The first question—where are they going?—is answered when we follow their procession to a nearby tree. The inch-long, orange-and-black caterpillars form lanes of two-way traffic up and down the trunk. At one point, they amass in a dinner-plate-size whorl that moves like a psychedelic pinwheel.

How they all knew where to go, and why they followed each other, underscores why one entomologist has described these eastern tent caterpillars as standing "at the pinnacle of sociality." The moth larvae strike out from their tent three times a day in search of food. On these solo forays, they lay down a pheromone called an "exploratory trail." Once a food source is found, the caterpillar eats and returns to the tent, leaving a "recruitment trail." This second trail is like a clarion call for other

KID APPEAL
Rent bikes at the visitor center and ride the easy, 3-mile High Point Multi-Use Trail (6-mile round-trip). Stop for a picnic lunch and play in the playground. Canoes and kayaks are available for rent, or bring your own to launch into Belmont Bay.

caterpillars, who follow the trail one after another until a line forms much like what we witnessed.

While considered a nuisance because they can defoliate entire trees, tent caterpillars are more a threat to orchards than the mature woodlands of Mason Neck. In the forests along Eagle Spur Trail, there are signs of a more serious caterpillar threat. Here, biologists have wrapped tree trunks with burlap, meant to trap and kill the gypsy moth caterpillar. An outbreak of this exotic, a native to Europe and Asia, can lead to millions of acres of deforestation. The caterpillar sees the burlap as cover from predators; the rangers use it to trap and capture them.

There is a lot of woodland to protect on the entire Mason Neck peninsula. Of the roughly 10,000 acres that make up the Neck, more than 6,000 acres are protected by public parks and refuges. Mason Neck State Park is one piece of that web, covering 1,813 acres. This includes 2 miles of shoreline on Belmont and Occoquan Bays, which empty into the Potomac River.

> *The adjacent Mason Neck National Wildlife Refuge was the first in the country established for the protection of bald eagles. It was formed in 1969 out of 845 acres and now totals more than 2,200 acres.*

Canoe and kayak rentals on Belmont Bay

Mason Neck State Park

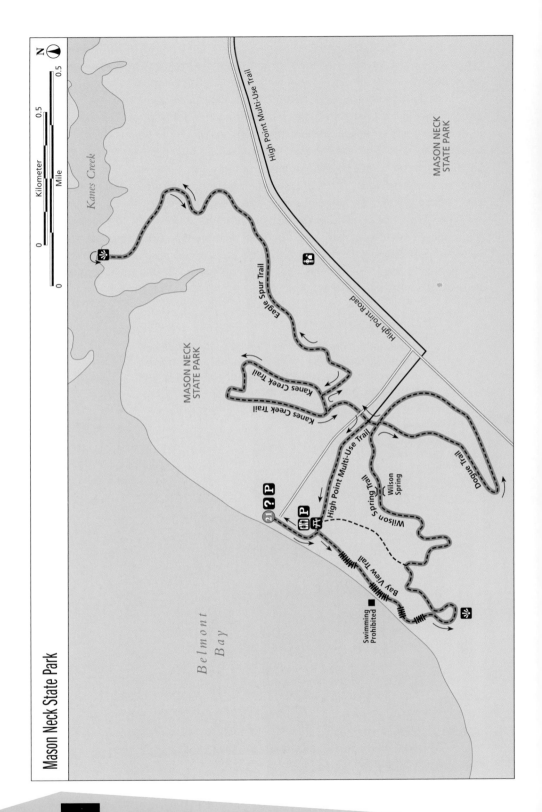

Kanes Creek

MASON NECK
STATE PARK

Belmont
Bay

Eagle Spur Trail

Kanes Creek Trail

Kanes Creek Trail

High Point Multi-Use Trail

High Point Road

Dogue Trail

Wilson Spring

Wilson Spring Trail

High Point Multi-Use Trail

Bay View Trail

Swimming
Prohibited

MASON NECK
STATE PARK

N

Kilometer
0   0.5

Mile
0   0.5

As you walk through the state park's oak forests, there are subtle signs of the historical use of this peninsula. Peninsulas like Mason Neck mark the Potomac River shoreline from Alexandria south. They were settled in the colonial period by wealthy planters, whose landholdings formed the basis of the colonial tobacco empire. Signs of tree clearing for fields is seen with the tulip poplars, of which so many fork into two large trunks about knee-high. After felling, the trees resprouted and turned into mature trees over decades of undisturbed growth.

Mason Neck's hiking trails are short. Not counting the paved High Point Multi-Use Trail, none of the park's six trails is more than 1.25 miles long. For a diversity of plant and animal life, the Bay View and Wilson Spring Trails are tops. These paths follow the shoreline of Belmont Bay, through a freshwater marsh, and into dry upland woods. Where it descends to the wet bottomland along seep that forms from Wilson Spring, the forest canopy closes in overhead. There's a musky scent, from skunk cabbage and other plants that love to get their feet wet.

Dogue Trail, a wide and graded path, features some of the park's largest trees. The American beech are especially impressive. This is the kind of tree that feels at home in any kind of forest, either as a tree that forms a canopy or as an understory tree in an oak/hickory forest. You can distinguish a beech while hiking in the winter and early spring. Their leaves, light, papery, and tan, stay on the tree throughout the winter, only to fall off when the new leaf buds push them off. Failing this, you might identify this tree by its tight gray bark (which is a perennial favorite of the initial-carving set).

If length is what you're after, Kanes Creek and Eagle Spur Trails combined offer the best option. Kanes Creek is a flat loop prone to washouts after a heavy rain. Eagle Spur is more varied, starting in dry oak and hickory woodland, passing into and out of small drainages marked by mountain laurel on the slopes, and finally ending at an overlook of Kanes Creek.

Or you can do them all together, as we did, and get a fair sampling of what a coastal forest looks, feels, and sounds like.

MILES AND DIRECTIONS

0.0 START from the state park visitor center. Walk around the building and turn left (west) on Bay View Trail, a gravel path. Belmont Bay is the open water on the right. After seventy steps, descend a flight of stairs, pass the cartop boat launch, and follow a boardwalk around a small pond.

0.1 Climb a set of stairs uphill and away from the pond. At the top, walk across a picnic area, using a wood fence as a handrail, and reenter the woods on the Bay View Trail. The graded path, lined with wood chips, is red blazed.

0.3 Descend a flight of stairs. Follow a boardwalk that spans an eroded shoreline on the right and an estuary on the left.

0.45 Detour right and descend to the shoreline of Belmont Bay. After exploring, return to the trail and follow a second boardwalk that spans the estuary.

0.55 Turn right on a spur trail that loops to an overlook. Bear right again when this spur trail forks.

0.6 Reach an overlook with limited summer views across the estuary.

0.65 Reach a blind with all-season views up into the freshwater reaches of the marsh. After a rest, resume walking the loop.

0.7 Bear right (north) at the junction with steps leading down to the boardwalk and begin a stretch of walking through dry upland forest. A profusion of blueberries and mountain laurel show strong rebound from a subcanopy fire in these woods in 1986.

0.8 Turn right on the yellow-blazed Wilson Spring Trail.

1.2 Cross a footbridge over Wilson Spring.

Boardwalk crosses a pond on the Bay View Trail

1.3 Turn right on Dogue Trail, a gravel-lined, handicapped-accessible trail.

2.1 Turn right on Wilson Spring Trail. Cross straight over High Point Trail, pass through a parking lot, and cross straight over the park road. On the other side, follow a boardwalk into the woods.

2.3 Two benches mark the Y junction with Kanes Creek Trail. Turn right on Kanes Creek, then take the next right onto Eagle Spur at a fork in the trail.

3.4 Reach an observation blind overlooking Kanes Creek. After a rest, retrace steps to the junction of Kanes Creek Trail.

4.5 Turn right onto Kanes Creek Trail. (**Bailout:** Veer left on Kanes Creek Trail, walk to the park road, and return to the park visitor center via High Point Trail.)

4.7 Pass an old trail on the right that is blocked by downed trees and marked with sensitive habitat warning signs. Kanes Creek Trail swings left. (**FYI:** The now-closed trail is the old access to Kanes Creek, which still appears on many maps and in guides. State conservation officials closed it to protect nesting bald eagles at the mouth of Kanes Creek.)

5.0 Turn right onto Wilson Spring Trail. Cross the park road and turn right on High Point Trail.

5.3 High Point junctions with the access road to the picnic and playground area. Turn left and follow the road. Pass bathrooms on the left, and then a trailboard sign.

There are more than 6,000 acres of protected land on Mason Neck out of a total land mass of 10,000 acres. State parks, wildlife refuges, regional parks, and historic plantations work cooperatively to create optimum conditions for nesting, mating, and roosting bald eagles.

5.4 At the edge of the bluff overlooking Belmont Bay, turn right and follow the trail back to the visitor center.

5.6 HIKE ENDS at the state park visitor center.

OPTIONS

Make this route an all-day trek by adding 6.6 miles via the High Point Multi-Use Trail and the neighboring refuge's Woodmarsh Trail. Where Wilson Spring Trail crosses High Point Road, turn right (east) and follow the paved multiuse trail 1.8 miles to the parking area and trailhead for Woodmarsh Trail. The refuge trail descends from hardwood forest to a marsh and includes an observation deck. If a bald eagle nest visible from the trail is active, portions of the route may be closed in late winter and early spring.

HIKE INFORMATION

Local information: Fairfax County/Capital Region Visitors Center, Tysons Corner Shopping Center, McLean, VA; (703) 752-9500; www.fxva.com

Local events/attractions: Mason Neck National Wildlife Refuge, 14344 Jefferson Davis Hwy., Woodbridge, VA; (703) 490-4979; www.fw.gov
The park holds the Liz Hartwell Eagle Festival in Apr and the Old Time Harvest Festival in Oct

Good eats: My Karma Indian Bistro, 9429 Lorton Market St., Lorton, VA; (703) 372-1888; www.mykarmabistro.com

Local outdoor stores: Modell's Sporting Goods, 6689 Springfield Mall, Springfield, VA; (703) 971-8303; www.modells.com

Hike tours: Park staff offer guided hikes and canoe trips in season

Organizations: Friends of Mason Neck, Lorton, VA; (703) 339-2385; www.dcr.virginia.gov/state_parks/mas.shtml

> 🌿 **Green Tip:**
> *Don't take souvenirs home with you. This means natural materials such as plants, rocks, shells, and driftwood as well as historic artifacts such as fossils and arrowheads.*

Overall Run, Shenandoah National Park

Peaks and waterfalls surely rank as prime motivators—and rewards—for a day spent hiking, and doubly so if you work hard to get there. There are no shortages of waterfalls in Shenandoah National Park, from the wildly popular Whiteoak Canyon to the Rose River Falls, where multiple cascades flow off bare-faced rock after heavy rains. But there's only one "tallest": 93 feet to be exact, and it's found on the western slope of the Blue Ridge at Overall Run. From the staggering falls, the mountainous panorama unfolds westward over Massanutten's double ridges, and farther off on the hazy horizon looms Great North Mountain.

Start: From the Thompson Hollow Trail parking area on VA 630, 2.5 miles south of Bentonville, Virginia
Distance: 6 miles out-and-back, with an option for an 11.5-mile loop
Approximate hiking time: 4 hours
Difficulty: Moderate due to unaided stream crossings and a vigorous climb to the top of the Overall Run headwall
Trail surface: A brief stint on paved and gravel road leads to the park boundary. From there on it's single-track woodland paths interrupted by three stream crossings and an opportunity to rock-scramble near the lip of the Overall Run falls.
Seasons: Best in autumn, winter, and spring for color and views— and fewer humans
Other trail users: Hikers only
Canine compatibility: Leashed dogs permitted
Land status: National park

Fees and permits: None since this trailhead is located outside the park
Schedule: Park is open 24 hours; headquarters is open Mon through Fri 8:00 a.m. to 4:30 p.m.
Facilities: None at this access point
Maps: DeLorme *Virginia Atlas & Gazetteer:* Page 74 B2. USGS 7.5 minute series: *Bentonville, VA.* See also the Potomac Appalachian Trail Club (PATC) Map #9 (*Shenandoah National Park: Northern District*).
Trail contacts: Shenandoah National Park, 3655 US 211 E., Luray, VA 22835; (540) 999-3500; www.nps.gov/shen
Special considerations: Winter is a spectacular time to visit, with huge ice sheets forming on the cliff. During the coldest snaps the falls may even be frozen solid. But be extremely careful on slippery rocks and keep your distance from the edge: It's 93 feet straight down.

Where Piney River passes through a steep gorge, the trail steepens as well, climbing the hillside on switchbacks. Where it briefly levels, the river can be heard but not seen. A small window through the forest canopy does offer a glimpse of the solid cliff wall on the opposite side. Just the spot, perhaps, a denning bear or a mountain lion might prefer.

The presence of mountain lions—also referred to as cougars, pumas, panthers, and catamounts—is subject to debate. Officially, the last eastern subspecies of mountain lion, *Felis concolor cougar*, was documented in Virginia in 1882. But sightings, if not actual documentation, are commonplace. A national park resource management newsletter in 1997 stated that reliable reports of mountain lion sightings had been made in the park since 1932. Whether the population is a resurgence of the native eastern cougar, a wanderer from another region (Florida currently has the only population of cougars in the East, the highly endangered Florida panther, *Felis concolor cory*), or an escaped or released pet, is unknown.

KID APPEAL

The Bolen family cemetery at the junction of Hull School Trail and Keyser Run Fire Road is a great teaching opportunity. Life in the Blue Ridge Mountains before the park was created was one of subsistence farming—in which nearly everything that was needed was provided by the land.

Author at stream

Any thought of a lurking predator is dispelled as you climb away from the Piney River gorge along Pole Bridge Link Trail. In spring, the grassy fringes of this trail are a spectacle of wildflowers, whether the ephemeral spring beauty, the white petals of giant chickweed, delicate purple wild geranium, or common violet and buttercup. Dry, grassy spots host a profusion of common lousewort, a red-and-yellow blossom that seems more at home in a cow pasture than these woodlands.

The descent through Little Devil Stairs offers what Piney Branch Trail only hinted at: up-close interaction with rugged nature. There are at least eight stream crossings, and, after a heavy rain, probably more. At one point, the cliffs on either side close in so tightly, you're forced to walk down a small island that conveniently emerges from the stream.

A rock talus marking the halfway point of the descent through Little Devil Stairs highlights the geologic dynamism of the park. A "river" of its own sort, the talus covers the hillside with rocks and boulders, most of them the size of tires or smaller. *Talus creep* describes the slow downward movement of this rock slope toward the valley bottom. In a geologic time frame, this slope is considered dynamic and moving. The slope and the quartzite rock itself show no signs of the stability (lichen or vegetation) that was evident on the stone stream alongside Hull School Trail.

MILES AND DIRECTIONS

0.0 START from the Little Devil Stairs parking lot. Follow a gravel road uphill from the west end of the parking lot.

0.2 Swing right (north) on the fire road and walk past signs marking the boundary of Shenandoah National Park.

1.1 After a steady climb, enter a clearing that is the junction of Keyser Run Fire Road and Hull School Trail. The Bolen family cemetery is off to the right.

Bolen Family Cemetery

The Bolen family cemetery occupies the clearing called Jinny Gray Flats at the 90-degree bend in Keyser Run Fire Road, at the junction with Hull School Trail. A stone fence surrounds it. Upkeep of the cemetery is good, inviting passersby to swing open the wrought-iron gate and step inside. Some headstones are engraved, while others appear to be random stones from the woods—place markers as much as anything else. In total, there are fifty or more burials, according to a list of cemeteries compiled by Darwin Lambert in his book *The Undying Past of Shenandoah National Park*. Burials date to the late 1800s and early 1900s, with 1935 being the most recent.

3.0 A vigorous climb levels briefly, and the forest canopy opens to views of the imposing cliff face on the opposite stream bank. In the next 0.1 mile of trail, look for unmarked paths leading off the trail right to the river's edge.

3.3 Cross Piney River on stream rocks and start a steady uphill climb on Piney Branch Trail. The stream is now on your left side.

3.5 The trail levels briefly, and off the trail to the left is a primitive campsite.

4.2 Detour off the trail to the left to explore the cliff line that gives visual proof of the elevation you've gained in the last 1.2 miles.

4.6 Turn right (east) on Pole Link Bridge Trail. Level terrain off both sides indicates you are traversing across the flat top of a ridge.

4.7 Pass a primitive campsite off the trail to the right.

4.9 Stay straight on Pole Bridge Link Trail at a junction with Sugarloaf Trail on the left.

5.4 Reach Fourway, a junction with Keyser Run Fire Road and Little Devil Stairs. Cross the fire road diagonally left and reenter woods on Little Devil Stairs Trail. The trailhead is marked by a concrete trail marker.

5.7 Begin a series of five switchbacks that carry you down a steep slope into the Little Devil Stairs Canyon.

Rethinking the Blue Ridge Image

The story of the people who lived in the Blue Ridge prior to creation of Shenandoah National Park is under constant revision. In the 1930s, they were depicted as isolated, primitive, and uncouth—ripe for "civilizing," and their farming practices were held up as destructive to the landscape. In the last decade, archaeological work has led to a reevaluation.

The work of the Survey of Mountain Settlement, which concentrated its studies in three hollows on the eastern slope of the Blue Ridge—Nicholson, Corbin, and Weakley—unearthed products from Sears, Roebuck & Co., such as toy ray guns that invoked memories of the Buck Rogers craze during the Depression, phonographic records, imported ceramic plates, and brass beds, which indicate there was plenty of interaction with the world outside their mountain hollows.

Reinterpreting the image of the people who settled the hollows of the Blue Ridge is an ongoing process. Created as a "natural" park, Shenandoah is now coming full circle to embrace and exhibit the livelihoods of the very people it displaced.

5.8 Cross Keyser Run, the first of four unaided stream crossings over the next 0.3 mile. (**Caution:** The next 1.1 miles descend *extremely* technical terrain as you scurry across, squeeze through, drop down off, and hop across rocks and boulders that litter this stream gorge.)

6.0 Cross Keyser Run for the fourth time and pass beneath a twenty-story-high cliff line that forms the right stream bank of the canyon. A talus in this area is littered with tire-size rocks, and the trail footbed is loose rubble.

6.1 Two quick stream crossings put you back on the right stream bank. Ahead, Keyser Run is squeezed by cliffs, and the trail takes a middle course down an island formed by a split in the stream. Watch for blue blazes on trees for guidance. (**Caution:** In spring or after heavy rainfall, this section may be washed out and require you to ford downstream as you follow the blue trail blazes.)

6.3 Cross Keyser Run from the right to the left stream bank. This is the first of four stream crossings as the trail emerges from the gorge into a wider stream valley.

6.7 Cross from the left to the right stream bank, the last in this dizzying descent. Ahead, the trail separates from the streamside and crosses a small knoll.

7.2 Begin a long flat stretch of hiking across flat bottomland forest. Just before reaching the trailhead parking lot, cross a stream.

7.4 HIKE ENDS at the Little Devil Stairs parking lot at the end of VA 614/Keyser Run Road.

HIKE INFORMATION

Local information: Rappahannock County Office of Tourism, Washington, VA; (540) 675-5330; www.visitrappahannockva.com

Local events/attractions: Wilderness Weekend is held each Oct at the park's Byrd Visitor Center, mile 51 on Skyline Drive, near Big Meadows

Good eats: Thornton River Grille, 3710 Sperryville Pike, Sperryville, VA; (540) 987-8790; www.thorntonrivergrille.com

Local outdoor stores: Blue Ridge Mountain Sports, 251 W. Lee Hwy., Warrenton, VA; (540) 428-3136; www.brmsstore.com

Hike tours: Park rangers lead a variety of nature, wildflower, and geology hikes Apr through Labor Day

Organizations: Potomac Appalachian Trail Club (PATC), Vienna, VA; (703) 242-0693; www.potomacappalachian.org

Prince William Forest Park

Prince William Forest Park was one of forty-six recreation demonstration projects dating to the Great Depression of the 1930s that restored land considered unprofitable for farming. Civilian Conservation Corps workers planted trees and stabilized stream banks, built camps, and laid out roads. The CCC's "make-work" purpose reaped a practical result: It demonstrated that land considered to be largely worthless could be reclaimed for public recreation and enjoyment. Today, the park is one of Northern Virginia's largest woodlands, with 37 miles of hiking trails and 12 miles of roads for biking. As you walk stream valley trails, pass by beaver-created wetlands, and listen to wood thrushes sing in the forest, you can chalk up this Depression-era experiment as a success.

Start: From the Laurel Loop Trail map board behind Pine Grove picnic pavilion

Distance: 15.6-mile loop with three shorter options

Approximate hiking time: 5 to 6 hours

Difficulty: Difficult due to length. Trails are well graded, clearly marked, and have only moderate elevation change.

Trail surface: Combination of dirt path, dirt road, forested trail, gravel road, boardwalk, and footbridges

Seasons: May and June, when mountain laurel blooms in profusion

Other trail users: Joggers, cross-country skiers. Bicycles are allowed on paved roads and fire roads.

Handicapped accessibility: The visitor center, campgrounds, and amphitheater are handicapped accessible. Pine Grove Forest Trail is an easy, 0.4-mile loop along a smooth boardwalk that features a wildlife-viewing platform and seating area. From Parking Area D, the park's paved Scenic Drive is one-way to vehicles, leaving an entire lane for strollers, joggers, and wheelchairs.

Canine compatibility: Leashed dogs permitted

Land status: National park

Fees and permits: Entrance fee (good for 7 days, when paid per vehicle)

Schedule: Park is open daily dawn to dusk. The visitor center is open daily 9:00 a.m. to 5:00 p.m.

Facilities: Restrooms at the visitor center and picnic areas. The visitor center features a wildlife exhibit. There is primitive camping and cabins for rent.

Maps: DeLorme *Virginia Atlas & Gazetteer:* Page 76 D3. USGS 7.5 minute series: *Quantico, VA* and *Joplin, VA.* The park gives out free brochures with park maps and roads depicted. Also, a binder in the visitor center has pages of hiking options, and rangers are nearby to give advice.

Trail contacts: Prince William Forest Park, 18100 Park Headquarters Rd., Triangle, VA 22172-1644; (703) 221-7181; www.nps.gov/prwi

Other: This is a "trash-free" national park: There are no garbage cans, so all trash must be packed out. The visitor center can supply garbage bags if needed.

Finding the trailhead:

Distance from Washington, D.C.: 34 miles

From I-95: Take exit 150 (Joplin Road/VA 619). At the bottom of the exit ramp, turn west on VA 619. Drive 0.4 mile and turn right into Prince William Forest Park. In 0.5 mile, turn left at a sign for Pine Grove Picnic Area. Immediately turn right into the long-term parking area. Walk up the small knoll and locate the Laurel Loop Trail map board at the edge of the woods between the Pine Grove Picnic Area and the visitor center. Trailhead GPS: N38 33.644' / W77 20.943'

THE HIKE

Themes of disturbance and renewal crop up seemingly at every turn as you explore Prince William Forest Park. First, there is the park itself, 15,000 acres that protect nearly the entire watershed of Quantico Creek. It was considered unprofitable land for farming when the federal government removed 150 families from the area to create the park's predecessor, the Chopawamsic Recreational Demonstration Area. Since the 1930s, natural succession has taken hold and returned the park to a prized example of Piedmont forest.

In this state, other types of disturbances now occur, natural ones like wildfires and floods, each a reminder that in nature's balancing act, renewal nearly always follows catastrophe.

Perched as it is on the fall line—a natural boundary between the Piedmont and Coastal Plain—the park straddles two natural worlds. A mile-long stretch of the North Valley Trail along Quantico Creek nicely sums up the transition: Where you descend off the Quantico Falls Trail and turn downstream to walk the North Valley Trail, a granite rock shelf extends out into the stream. Several low-grade falls and rapids form downstream. Where the stream narrows and the banks become sheer, the trail is forced high up onto the hillsides, a wonderful opportunity to walk through thick groves of mountain laurel, which blooms here in May and June.

Soon the stream valley opens up, and the trail passes through a wide area of river bottomland. The terrain is flat, and the birch, tulip poplar, and sycamore trees are younger. The biggest change, however, is beneath your feet, where the earth is now the sandy soil typical of the Coastal Plain.

In recent years, signs of natural disturbance are dramatic along the North Valley and South Valley Trails. Effects of flooding mar the stream's bottomland forest. In particular, a period of heavy rainfall in spring 2008 left its mark. Floodwaters swept dead branches, leaves, and other forest debris downstream. Small footbridges for hikers were uprooted. Tree logs taller and thicker than telephone poles

> *Of the forty-six recreation demonstration projects created by the Department of the Interior and the Civilian Conservation Corps, many have become state parks. Others, however, include some of our most recognizable national parks, including Acadia in Maine, Badlands in South Dakota, and, of note to metro D.C. residents, Catoctin Mountain Park in Maryland.*

South Fork Quantico Creek

were moved hundreds of yards to land at odd angles far from the stream. Wherever this accumulated mass of debris hit an obstacle, like a fallen tree that spanned the creek from one bank to the other, the damming created a dramatic rise in water that spilled over into the creek's floodplain.

Another natural disturbance is found near Oak Ridge Campground, where the South Valley Trail rises away from verdant wetlands formed by beaver dams into drier forest where trunks of the oak and pine trees are charred and blackened. Wide swaths of felled trees have formed clearings, and there are cut logs stacked and piled. This was the site of a wildfire in March and April of 2006, when a camper's error led to burning of 318 acres of the park's forestland.

In the years since the floods and fires, renewal has followed. The stream bottomland that flooded has, on closer inspection, the look of a recently plowed-over field. Plants and tree saplings are bent in half, resembling images of the aftermath of a hurricane. The accumulation of debris around their trunks further enhances their frozen-in-time illusion. The loose crumbly topsoil of the floodplain is fertile ground for new trees and plants.

Biologists at Prince William Forest Park are paying close attention to the white pines in the burnt forest. This conifer's cones are serotinous, which means they remain closed on the tree until a stressor—in this case, intense heat from fire—causes them to open and drop their seedlings.

While the floods and fires are the most dramatic, there are countless other small disturbances where hikers can see the process of renewals. When a storm knocks down a few trees to create a small forest clearing, grass quickly takes root in the patch of sunshine. Small beetles and spiders begin the long process of decomposing fallen deadwood. Their activity attracts birds, including pileated and red-headed woodpeckers as well as songbirds, looking to feast on the small insect life. A shrub layer of spicebush will give way to young tree saplings—maybe maple or ironwood.

In these clearings, it is possible to imagine how Prince William Forest Park started its long road toward becoming the mature woodland it is today.

MILES AND DIRECTIONS

0.0 START from the Laurel Loop Trail map board behind the Pine Grove picnic pavilion. Do not enter the woods here, but rather turn left (north) and follow a narrow well-worn dirt path through a grassy area. You'll pass a playground and then enter a field at the far end of a paved parking lot. Walk down the right side of the field, keeping the woods hard to your right. In the far northeast corner of the field, locate the yellow blazes for the alternate Laurel Loop trailhead. The trail here is a wide, graded dirt path. The trailhead is marked by a yellow blaze on a tulip poplar and a concrete trail post with a metal band that gives the trail's name and mileage to the next junction.

Prince William Forest Park

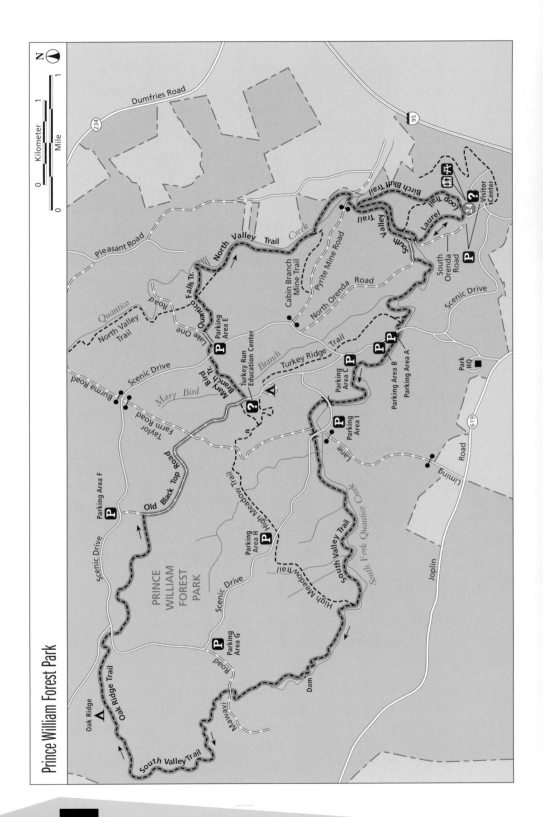

0.4 Continue straight ahead on the Laurel Loop Trail at a junction with a short spur trail on the left that descends left to South Orenda Road.

0.5 Turn left (west) and cross the South Fork Quantico Creek on a cable-supported bridge. On the opposite side, turn left (west) on a dirt road that is the combined South Valley Trail and North Orenda Road. (**Bailout:** Don't cross the bridge; instead, bear right and follow a combination of Laurel Loop and Birch Bluff Trail to return to the Pine Grove picnic area for a quick 2-mile loop.)

0.7 Turn left (south) on South Valley Trail as it splits off North Orenda Road.

1.4 Stay straight at a T junction with Turkey Run Ridge Trail. Ahead, South Valley Trail winds through bottomland forest formed by a bend in the stream, and then turns north.

1.5 Bear left on South Valley Trail. (**Note:** The trail straight ahead becomes Turkey Run Ridge Trail where the cutoff from 1.4 miles merges on the right.) (**Bailout:** For a 6.15-mile loop, follow Turkey Run Ridge Trail [dark blue blazes] uphill to the Turkey Run Education Center, and return to Pine Grove via Mary Bird Branch, Quantico Falls, and North Valley Trails.)

1.6 Cross over Scenic Drive. (**Note:** This is a reroute of South Valley Trail built to replace a washout-prone route.)

2.1 Cross a footbridge over a small stream. After a strong rainfall, this tributary of the South Fork is a bubbling, cascading treat. Ahead, South Valley Trail climbs a hillside on switchbacks.

2.6 Cross beneath Scenic Drive via a boardwalk that hugs the concrete bridge abutment.

2.8 Stay straight on South Valley Trail at a junction with Taylor Farm Road on the right. (**Bailout:** For an 8.8-mile loop, turn right on Taylor Farm Road and use the High Meadow Trail to return to Turkey Run Education Center, and then back to Pine Grove picnic area via Mary Bird Branch, Quantico Falls, and North Valley Trails.)

KID APPEAL

The 1.4-mile Laurel Loop Trail is easily reached from the Pine Grove picnic area, where there is also a playground. The forested path gets you down to the stream quickly for some water play.

2.9   Cross over Scenic Drive and continue west on the South Valley Trail.

4.4   Turn left (west) and follow South Valley Trail downhill at this junction with High Meadow Trail, which continues straight uphill. In the next 0.75 mile, you will make three short, steep climbs from the river-bottom forest to hillside forests as the South Fork Quantico Creek narrows and twists through tight, steep terrain. (**Note:** In May, when its white blossoms show, mountain laurel crowd this section of trail, making it one of the most scenic in the park.)

5.2   Pass a dam across the South Fork. Above this, the creek spreads out to form a long, narrow lake.

6.0   Cross over gravel Mawavi Road and walk north on South Valley Trail up the stream valley.

6.4   Enter wetlands where, for the next 0.7 mile, the trail skirts an area of heavy beaver activity. This wet, wide open ecosystem attracts waterfowl, songbirds, deer, raccoon, and fox.

7.1   Begin a climb from the stream valley into dry upland forest of chestnut oak, yellow (tulip) poplar, and white oak that is in recovery from a 2006 wildfire that consumed 318 acres.

8.0   Turn right (east) on the yellow-blazed Oak Ridge Trail.

Mountain laurel blooms are prolific in May

8.5 Cross straight over Scenic Drive.

9.2 After a level stretch of hiking through a young upland forest, descend into a small stream valley with a moist forest understory of fern and skunk cabbage.

9.5 Oak Ridge Trail ends at a T junction with Old Black Top Road. Turn right (south) and walk along the gravel road.

10.4 At a four-way junction with Taylor Farm Road, continue straight on Old Black Top Road.

10.9 Turn left (north) onto Mary Bird Branch Trail. There is a concrete trail post and a triple red blaze on a tree. Ahead, descend and cross Mary Bird Branch, a stream.

11.3 Cross straight over Scenic Drive and pass through the parking and picnic area E. Locate a white signboard for Quantico Falls Trail. Enter the woods on a footpath following yellow blazes. (**Note:** You'll periodically see brown trail blazes and trailside signs for the Geology Trail, which shares the trail from here to Quantico Creek.)

11.4 Turn left onto a dirt road. Stay alert when, in less than 0.1 mile, Quantico Falls Trail branches right off the dirt road. Turn right here and follow the yellow-blazed trail through an upland deciduous forest of oak and hickory with an understory of beech, maple, and elm.

11.8 Cross over the North Valley Trail at a four-way trail junction.

12.0 A sharp descent ends at the edge of Quantico Creek. Turn right (south) and follow the stream valley. There are a scenic set of waterfalls off to the left.

12.2 Cross a footbridge over a small tributary and merge with the blue-blazed North Valley Trail. Veer left (south) and walk downstream. (**FYI:** In summer and fall, the trail south of this junction offers good opportunities to rest and relax on exposed rock shelves in the river.)

12.9 Pass interpretive signs for the Cabin Branch pyrite mine, which operated on Quantico Creek in the early 1900s.

13.0 Cross Quantico Creek on a bridge. On the opposite side, turn right to follow a footpath through river-bottom forest. (**Side trip:** Before crossing the creek, walk straight ahead to another section of the pyrite mine in less than 0.1 mile.)

13.2 A long boardwalk carries the trail over a wetland. Ahead, look for an overlook on the right that gives you a vantage point of the Cabin Branch mine across the stream.

13.5 After walking a short stretch on gravel road, turn right (west) and cross Quantico Creek on a bridge. On the opposite side, turn left (west) onto South Valley Trail.

14.1 Turn left (south) and cross South Fork Quantico Creek on a cable-supported bridge. Bear left at two trail junctions on the right.

14.3 At a T-junction with a trail on the right, stay straight on red-blazed Birch Bluff Trail, which continues as a dirt footpath alongside the creek. (**Note:** The right turn here is the return leg of Laurel Loop.)

15.3 Swing left and follow a clear wide trail at a double red blaze.

15.5 Double red blazes mark a hard right in the trail. Pass through a wooded strip and reach a concrete trail post. Turn left (north) at the post and walk this last leg of the Laurel Loop.

15.6 HIKE ENDS at the Pine Grove picnic area.

Cabin Branch Pyrite Mine

The woods of Prince William Forest Park are quiet save for bird calls and the wind rustling leaves, but from 1889 to 1920 the Cabin Branch pyrite mine was in full swing. Sometimes called fool's gold for its luster, pyrite was a cost-efficient source of sulfur that was used to make paper, rubber, medicine, and explosives. During this time, which included World War I, when pyrite miners were exempt from military conscription, Cabin Branch produced more than 224,000 tons for U.S. industry. Bringing the pyrite to the surface was dangerous business, and many men died in the process. Children worked for 50 cents a day sorting the pyrite rocks by size. When miners went on strike for higher wages, the owner closed the mine instead.

OPTIONS

Our goal was to plot a route through Prince William Forest Park that maximized its 37 miles of trails as well as its diverse natural habitats. The 15.6-mile hike described above provides three bailout options that reduce the length and difficulty. Laurel Loop (2 miles) is the shortest and easiest, and it can be done in an hour or less. The Turkey Run Ridge option (6.15 miles) is moderate due to length. An 8.8-mile route using Taylor Farm Road and the High Meadow Trail offers an interesting walk through meadows that are reverting to woodland. The full hike of 15.6 miles takes you to the farthest reaches of the park.

HIKE INFORMATION

Local information: Prince William County Visitor Information Center, 200 Mill St., Occoquan, VA; (703) 491-4045; www.visitpwc.com

Local events/attractions: Old Mine Ranch, 7504 Mine Rd., P.O. Box 10, Dumfries, VA; (703) 441-1382; www.oldmineranch.net. Working farm offers pony rides, petting farm, and western theme town.

Good eats: Tim's Rivershore Restaurant & Crabhouse, 1510 Cherryhill Rd., Dumfries, VA; (703) 441-1375; www.timsrivershore.com. Enjoy fresh seafood and a view of the Potomac River.

Local outdoor stores: Modell's Sporting Goods, Potomac Mills, Woodbridge, VA; (703) 499-9696; www.modells.com

Hike tours: Park staff offer nature programs and orienteering classes

Organizations: Friends of Prince William Forest Park, Woodbridge, VA; (703) 791-2282; www.fpwfp.org

🌿 **Green Tip:**
Observe wildlife from a distance. Don't interfere in their lives—both of you will be better for it. If an animal interrupts its activity and looks at you, chances are you've gotten too close.

Riverbend Park

This small, compact Fairfax County park sits on a deep bend in the Potomac River north of Great Falls and protects some of the globally rare natural communities that have in recent years made the Potomac Gorge a hot spot for naturalists. Terrain is diverse, ranging from riverside floodplain to upland forests. There is a trail through hilltop meadows excellent for bird-watching. Only the Potomac Heritage Trail along the river is longer than 2 miles, but several of the park's shorter trails can be strung together for a walk that, while lacking in distance and endurance, exceeds in natural beauty.

Start: From the park nature center

Distance: There are 10 miles of trails in the park, with options to link with Great Falls Park to the south

Approximate hiking time: 1 to 3 hours

Difficulty: Easy due to gentle terrain and short, well-marked trails

Trail surface: Forested trails, dirt riverside paths, paved roads, gravel paths

Seasons: Best in winter and spring. Many species of wildflowers thrive along the riverbank from Mar to June, and Virginia bluebell is especially prolific along the wooded trails.

Other trail users: Mountain bikers, equestrians, anglers

Handicapped accessibility: The Duff 'N' Stuff Trail is a 0.25-mile-long paved trail near the nature center. Paved roads and sidewalks descend from the visitor center to the river's edge.

Canine compatibility: Leashed dogs permitted

Land status: County park

Fees and permits: None

Schedule: Daily 7:00 a.m. to dusk

Facilities: Restrooms, picnic shelter and picnic area, visitor center, nature center, gift shop, snack bar

Maps: DeLorme *Virginia Atlas & Gazetteer:* Page 80 D3. USGS 7.5 minute series: *Rockland, MD/VA.*

Trail contacts: Riverbend Park, 8700 Potomac Hills St., Great Falls, VA 22066; (703) 759-9018; www.fairfaxcounty.gov/parks/riverbend Friends of Riverbend Park, www.forb.org. A volunteer group that advocates for the park.

Special considerations: As Riverbend is part of a Globally Rare Environment, it is illegal to pick or otherwise harm plant life in the park

Finding the trailhead:

Distance from Washington, D.C.: 19 miles

From I-495 (Capital Beltway): Take exit 44 (Georgetown Pike/VA 193). Drive west on Georgetown Pike, and in 4.5 miles turn right onto Riverbend Road. In 2.1 miles, turn right onto Jeffery Road. Stay straight on Jeffery Road past an intersection with Potomac Hills Street, following signs for Riverbend Park Nature Center. (*Note:* A right turn onto Potomac Hills Street leads to the park's visitor center.) Bear hard right as Jeffery Road bends east, avoiding River Birch Drive, which goes straight. In 1.3 miles from Riverbend Road, Jeffery Road ends at a parking lot for the nature center. Trailhead GPS: N39 01.330' / W77 15.002'

THE HIKE

The Potomac River's watershed drains nearly 15,000 square miles of land, from the Allegheny Highlands of western Pennsylvania all the way to the Chesapeake Bay. Its highest elevations are rugged peaks in West Virginia. The rivers and streams that drain eastward off the Allegheny Plateau originate in boreal bogs more typical of alpine Canadian climates. At Harpers Ferry, the Potomac cuts through the Blue Ridge Mountains and, after receiving the Shenandoah River, settles into a wide course through Piedmont farmlands. The southern bank marks the boundary between Maryland and Virginia. Great Falls marks the river's drop into flat land of the Coastal Plain, where the river is influenced by Chesapeake Bay tides. From there on, for more than 110 miles, the Potomac follows a serpentine course to its confluence with the Chesapeake Bay.

From time preceding English settlement of Virginia up until today, the Potomac River has influenced travel and settlement, trade and commerce, culture and recreation. Its role as a thread through different geographic regions and different eras helped inspire the Potomac Heritage National Scenic Trail (NST). Conceived in the 1970s, the trail is a route that strives to link not just the river's natural highlights, but the shared history of people and events along the river.

Small and compact, Riverbend's 402 acres preserve wooded bluffs whose forests are reminiscent of Appalachian cove forests. The hilltop meadows attract both birds and the people that watch them in all seasons. And along the floodplain of

KID APPEAL

Stroller-appropriate trails include the 0.25-mile asphalt Duff 'N' Stuff Trail that loops from the nature center into quiet, shady woods. There are also paved walks around the visitor center and down to the river. In summer, tractor-drawn wagon rides are offered to a remote area of the park.

the Potomac River, the park's longstanding River Trail offers hikers an easy, rambling route with views onto the Potomac River and its many islands. In 2007, this 2.5-mile route officially joined the Potomac Heritage NST network, making Riverbend Park part of the still-unfolding story of the Potomac's natural and cultural history.

The riverside trail is short and easy on the legs. There are plenty of opportunities to explore side routes that climb up into the hillside forests. Tall, thick-trunked sycamore trees line the river's edge, noticeable by their blotchy white and gray bark. The ephemeral wildflowers bloodroot and spring beauty emerge for a day

Capt. John Smith's 1608 exploration of the Chesapeake Bay and its tributaries brought him to the Great Falls of the Potomac. He and his crew hiked overland past the falls and encountered a tribe of Native Americans laden with bear, beaver, deer, and other meat. A crew member later wrote in his diary that they saw bison grazing. Archaeologists have documented over 11,000 years of Native American life at today's Riverbend Park, the most recent a tribe documented by Smith called the Nacotchtanks. The park's annual Virginia Indian Festival held each fall celebrates this Native American heritage.

Potomac River View

or two in spring, their white petals an uplifting sign of warmer weather. After a heavy spring rain, the trail is waterlogged at its low points. Spring peepers, a type of tree frog, raise a raucous chorus that quiets as your footsteps approach. Its call is a short, high-pitched whistle. A chorus of spring peepers sounds like a thousand jingle bells ringing, and on a quiet evening, it can be heard up to a mile away. These tiny frogs—their size is equivalent to your thumbnail—find shelter on the low branches of shrubs around a bog or wetland. It's telltale marking resembles a Christian cross, which inspired the frog's Latin name, *Pseudacris crucifer*.

Flooding is a fact of life along the Potomac River, and even more so at Riverbend Park. Water may rise higher and quicker at certain downstream locations, where the Potomac is squeezed into narrow Mather Gorge, but at Riverbend, a low-elevation, relatively flat, wide floodplain results in flooding five or six times a year. This in turn has given rise to peculiar landforms and plant communities. Hiking north from the visitor center, you'll pass Black Pond, a seemingly benign backswamp. In flood conditions, however, Black Pond becomes a chute—literally a troughlike shortcut for river water that has spilled over the bank and seeks the short route across the river bend.

At the north end of Black Pond, a rerouting of the Potomac Heritage NST diverts you away from a globally rare, environmentally sensitive plant community. The Nature Conservancy helped document the site as part of their ongoing research in what they've termed the Potomac Gorge region. The gorge is presently defined as a 15-mile stretch of the Potomac starting at Riverbend Park and ending at Theodore Roosevelt Island. The assemblage of terrain, from Riverbend's expansive floodplain to the 140-foot cliffs of Mathers Gorge, host a diversity of plant, animal, and insect life that is still being documented and interpreted. At Riverbend, biologists identified one particular kind of rare plant community north of Black Pond, an area of exposed rocks and woodland called a woodland scour. After a particularly violent flood, or if the land has been raked over by ice flows, this may look more like a scrubland scour. Willow and sycamore trees are dominant, with smaller green ash, river birch, and silver maple present as well. While characterized as a highly disturbed environment, it is the disturbance of flooding that makes it unique.

To accommodate this plant community, volunteers rerouted the Potomac Heritage NST just north of Black Pond. Where you once followed the riverside, hikers now veer left, cross a dry section of the Black Pond chute and then a small tributary stream, and climb to the top of a knoll. It is a nice, short diversion from the river's edge and provides winter and spring views out over the mighty Potomac. There is something comforting about watching the mass of water moving downriver. So,

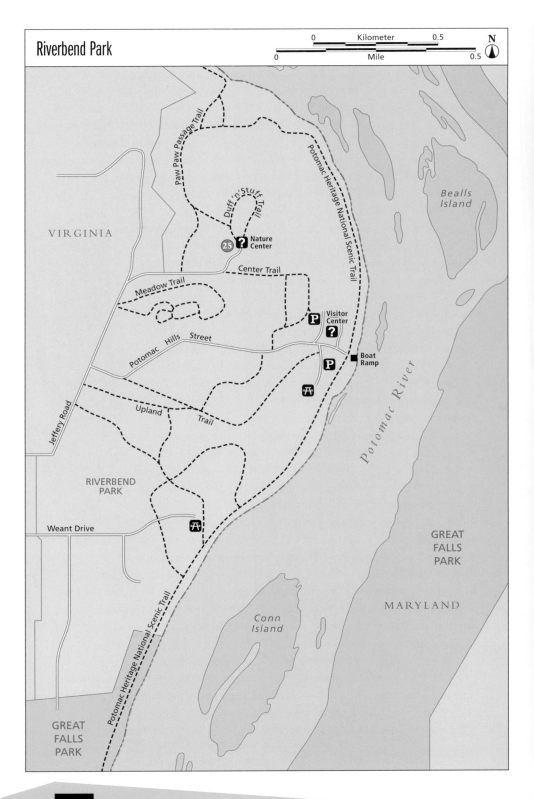

Riverbend Park

0   Kilometer   0.5

0   Mile   0.5

N

VIRGINIA

Paw Paw Passage Trail

Duff 'n' Stuff Trail

Potomac Heritage National Scenic Trail

Bealls Island

25   ? Nature Center

Center Trail

Meadow Trail

P   ? Visitor Center

Potomac Hills Street

P   Boat Ramp

Potomac River

Jeffery Road

Upland   Trail

RIVERBEND PARK

Weant Drive

GREAT FALLS PARK

MARYLAND

Conn Island

Potomac Heritage National Scenic Trail

GREAT FALLS PARK

too, is the thought that for as long as the Potomac has been flowing, we are still learning about just what makes this such a special river.

HIKE INFORMATION

Local information: Fairfax County/Capital Region Visitors Center, Tysons Corner Shopping Center, 2nd level, 1961 Chain Bridge Rd., McLean, VA; (703) 752-9500; www.fxva.com

Local events/attractions: Riverbend Park, Great Falls, VA; (703) 759-9018; ww.fairfaxcounty.gov/parks/riverbend. Hosts the Virginia Indian Festival each Sept.

Good eats: Deli Italiano Gourmet Pizza & Subs, 762-B Walker Rd., Great Falls, VA; (703) 759-6782

The Old Brogue, 762-C Walker Rd., Great Falls, VA; (703) 759-3309

Local outdoor stores: Hudson Trail Outfitters, 9488 Fairfax Blvd., Fairfax, VA; (703) 591-2950; www.hudsontrail.com

REI, 11950 Grand Commons Ave., Fairfax, VA; (571) 522-6568; www.rei.com

Dick's Sporting Goods, 12501 Fair Lakes Circle, Fairfax, VA; (703) 803-0300; www.dickssportinggoods.com

Hike tours: The park conducts wildflower walks in spring, particularly in mid-Apr when the Virginia bluebell blooms. In summer, there are tractor-drawn wagon

Paw Paw Blossoms

rides to a remote area of the park. Fishing guides and kayak tours are available May through Oct. Friends of Riverbend Park sponsor birding walks, mountain bike classes, fishing events, and kayak trips.

Organizations: Friends of Riverbend Park, Great Falls, VA; (703) 959-9018; www .forb.org

Potomac Appalachian Trail Club (PATC), Vienna, VA; **(703)** 242-0315; www .potomacappalachian.org

Other resources: Potomac Heritage National Scenic Trail, Harpers Ferry, WV; (304) 535-4014; www.nps.gov/pohe

The Threatened Wood Turtle

Already recognized for harboring a globally rare plant community—the woodland scour of the Potomac River floodplain—Riverbend Park also shelters a state-threatened reptile, the wood turtle. Park staff first documented this tortoise in 2008. Because it is known only in four Virginia counties, the state has listed it as a reptile whose existence is threatened. Biologists attribute its decline to habitat fragmentation, loss of wetlands, siltation of streams from human development, and collection by humans for the pet trade.

The wood turtle lacks flashy colors on its carapace (shell) like the similarly sized box turtle, but it does have one distinctive feature that could help you identify it. Look closely at the scutes (plates) on the turtle's carapace. A wood turtle's scutes down the center of the carapace are keeled; they literally rise up to a blunt point like small pyramids. This feature is the source of one of the turtle's nicknames: sculptured tortoise.

It lives both in dry forest and stream habitats, preferring the dry land during summer and moving to the stream in winter. Regardless of where it's found, the wood turtle always needs a stream or flooded wetland nearby to prevent drying out during heat spells.

One of its favorite food sources is fruit of the pawpaw tree, which means at Riverbend Park, as you walk the Paw Paw Passage Trail between the nature center and the Potomac River, you should keep a sharp eye and ear out for this small turtle scuffling through the leafy understory of the forest. If you see one, take a picture, note the location, and let park staff know about your discovery. Do not touch or otherwise disturb the turtles.

Sky Meadows State Park

On first approach, it's easy to see how Sky Meadows got its name and why amateur astronomers flock here to view the heavens. Hillside pastures offer expansive views in every direction. The views from Piedmont Overlook and the Ambassador Whitehouse Trails stir memories of alpine meadows. The Appalachian Trail passes through the park for 3 miles, and numerous house ruins and wagon roads tell the story of long-gone farmers.

Start: From a map trailboard 60 feet west of the visitor parking lot

Distance: 6.7-mile loop

Approximate hiking time: 3 hours

Difficulty: Moderate due to a mix of long uphill climbs through hillside meadows and level terrain along the ridge top. The forest trails are rocky with brief, but steep, inclines.

Trail surface: Forest trails, mowed meadow paths, gravel road

Seasons: Best Sept through Nov and Apr through June

Other trail users: Hikers only

Handicapped accessibility: Two dedicated parking spots. Bathrooms, the visitor center, and the gift shop are accessible via a paved path and ramp. One picnic site with a grill is accessible, as is a flat, but not paved, trail to the fishing pond.

Canine compatibility: Leashed dogs permitted

Land status: State park, National Scenic Trail

Fees and permits: Entrance fee; camping fee (allowed in desig-nated primitive sites only)

Schedule: Open daily 8:00 a.m. to dusk, including holidays. Visitor center hours: Wed through Sun 11:00 a.m. to 5:00 p.m. Park office hours: Mon through Fri 10:00 a.m. to 5:00 p.m.

Facilities: Restrooms, picnic tables, visitor center with small nature center and gift shop (sells firewood), beverage machine at picnic shelter

Maps: DeLorme *Virginia Atlas & Gazetteer:* Page 77 A5. USGS 7.5 minute series: Upperville, VA. See also National Geographic's TOPO! software, Mid-Atlantic Region, Disc 4: Washington, D.C. State park–issued trail maps are available at an interactive kiosk located in the picnic area next to the visitor center. A hand-drawn map is available online at www.dcr.virginia.gov/state_parks/sky.shtml.

Trail contacts: Sky Meadows State Park, 1102 Edmunds Lane, Delaplane, VA 20144; (540) 592-3556; www.dcr.virginia.gov/state_parks/sky.shtml
Potomac Appalachian Trail Club (PATC), 118 Park St. SE, Vienna, VA 22180; (703) 242-0315; www.potomacappalachian.org

Special considerations: This is a fairly dry hike. There's nowhere to hide from the blistering summer sun while hiking through the park's hilly meadows. Gap Run is the only stream of any reliability. There is a well at the primitive campsite, but water must be treated before used for drinking.

Finding the trailhead:
Distance from Washington, D.C.: 60 miles
From I-66: Take exit 23, following signs for US 17/VA 55 and Delaplane. Continue straight (north) on US 17 when VA 55 turns left (west). In 6.7 miles, turn left (west) on CR 710 (Edmunds Lane) and enter the state park. It is 0.5 mile on CR 710 to the park contact station, and 1.1 miles to the visitor center and trailhead parking. Trailhead GPS: N38 59.527' / W77 57.997'

THE HIKE

The impressive stone Mount Bleak House greets you when you pull into the parking lot, a tangible reminder that this young park is steeped in history. The famous philanthropist Paul Mellon donated the original property of 1,132 acres in 1975 expressly for development as a state park. In 1987, 245 acres were added for access to the Appalachian Trail, and in 1988, Mellon topped it off with another 486 acres.

The view inspired a resident of Mount Bleak during World War II to name it Skye Farm, in tribute to his native Isle of Skye in Scotland, and so the park became Sky Meadows.

The entire area of Loudoun County drips with the Civil War, with much of it focused around Col. John Singleton Mosby and his "rangers." He dominated this area during the Civil War so much that the surrounding countryside was dubbed "Mosby's Confederacy."

On the morning of July 19, 1861, Abner Settle of Mount Bleak would have seen thousands of Union campfires, the soldiers camped there on their way to the First Battle of Bull Run (Manassas). Two of the Settle boys were among Mosby's Rangers.

Today, a line of replica cannon recalls those solemn times. Nearby, a trailboard lifts the mood. We're here for hiking, after all, not to re-hash old battles.

Begin walking on a dirt road built in the 1820s to connect the 3 miles between the village of Paris and Semper's Mill. Deeply rutted by wagon wheels, the road is flanked by fieldstone fences with cornfields and pastures beyond them.

The road leads to Snowden Manor, the ruins of which can still be seen. Here George S. Ayre lived with his wife and four daughters. A sign tells the sad tale: In summary, the last of the girls died here, an old woman in 1893. The house was sold for debts in 1902, and in 1913 the frame house burned, leaving the brick chimney and the flagstone foundations we see today.

Prolific spring wildflowers and naturalized daffodils lining the trail lift the mood again. In a little over 2 miles you reach the Appalachian Trail (AT), a trail sign helpfully informing you that Harper's Ferry, West Virginia, is only 32.8 miles to go! On this footpath highway you're as likely to meet grubby through-hikers on a 2,000-mile journey as you are day-tripping urbanites on a Saturday trail run.

The park's focal point, Mount Bleak House (in this case, bleak means "exposed to the weather"), was built in the 1840s by Abner and Mary Settle. The journal of their niece, Amanda Edmonds, gives a firsthand account of Civil War–era events that took place here. It is for sale in the gift shop.

Headed for some high meadow hiking

light-blue–blazed junction. The trail reenters the woods and descends via switchbacks.

6.0   At a North Ridge Trail junction, turn left (east), descend 88 yards, and turn left (north) again onto the red-blazed Piedmont Overlook Trail. Within 0.1 mile, cross a fence stile and enter a spacious meadow.

6.4   After a long descent through the hillside meadows, the trail turns hard right and crosses a footbridge. There is an old livestock barn on the right.

6.6   At a North Ridge Trail junction, turn left (south), cross a fence stile, and descend to the gravel road (Gap Run Trail). Turn left again and walk 150 feet north to a red metal gate, where you turn right (east).

6.7   HIKE ENDS at the map board adjacent to the visitor parking lot.

> *Look for red-headed woodpeckers foraging in the oak trees around the visitor center. Six other species of woodpeckers also live in the park: downy, hairy, red-bellied, yellow-bellied sapsucker, pileated, and northern flicker.*

Appalachian Trail day-hikers

OPTIONS

You can shorten this loop by 1.3 miles by skipping the Old Trail and staying straight (north) on the AT to its junction with the Ambassador Whitehouse Trail. Or, if you're in the mood for an open-air meadow hike, focus on the Piedmont Overlook Trail (0.6 mile), Ambassador Whitehouse Trail (1.1 miles), and the lower half of the North Ridge Trail.

HIKE INFORMATION

Local information: Warrenton-Fauquier Visitor's Center, 33 N. Calhoun St., Warrenton, VA; (800) 820-1021; www.visitfauquier.com. Provides dining, museum, winery, and lodging information.

Local events/attractions: Astronomy Evenings at Sky Meadows State Park, Apr through Nov; admission fee. Civil War interpretive programs also take place throughout the year. The park hosts the Virginia Scottish Games in mid-Sept. Call (540) 592-3556 for a schedule of events.

Good eats: Hunter's Head Tavern, 9048 John Mosby Hwy. (US 50), Upperville, VA; (540) 592-9020; www.huntersheadtavern.com. English-themed pub in a 1750 log cabin with Guinness on tap, fish-and-chips, and hearty, crusty bread. The pub menu is half price from 3:00 to 6:00 p.m.

Local outdoor stores: Mountain Trails, 212 E. Cork St., Winchester, VA; (540) 667-0030; www.mountain-trails.com

Hike tours: Park rangers and volunteers lead butterfly, full moon, and wildflower walks. Tours of Mount Bleak House are given Sat, Sun, and major holidays from 1:00 to 4:00 p.m. mid-Apr through Oct. A self-guided walking tour brochure of the buildings of the Mount Bleak Historic Area is available in the visitor center.

Organizations: The Mosby Heritage Area Association, Middleburg, VA; (540) 687-6681; www.mosbyheritagearea.org

---

🐾 Green Tip:
When hiking with your dog, stay in the center of the path and keep Fido close by. Dogs that run loose can harm fragile soils and spread pesky plants by carrying their seeds.

This figure-eight-styled hike touches on all aspects of the varied terrain within this compact Nature Conservancy landholding. A steep walk up the mountain slope aided by thirteen switchbacks puts you atop England Mountain, with stirring winter and spring views west to North Marshall Mountain in Shenandoah National Park. Throughout the preserve, the trails and forest roads meander casually through former pastureland returning to forest. Note the labor required to create the numerous beautiful stone walls throughout. Take a break on the lawn of the Old Smith House and imagine those who lived and worked here a century ago. The naturalized daffodils around the perimeter serve as a bittersweet reminder of the long-ago efforts to bring early spring color to winter's bleakness.

Start: From a gravel parking lot and trail signboard on a private road off England Mountain Road.

Distance: 5.1-mile loop

Approximate hiking time: 3 hours

Difficulty: Moderate due to several steep climbs

Trail surface: The first 0.5 mile is a steep forest path uphill. Old dirt farm roads characterize the trails through the upland hardwood forest.

Seasons: Best in winter and early spring

Other trail users: Cross-country skiers, horseback riders

Handicapped accessibility: Access is limited to a few hundred feet of gravel road north of the parking area

Canine compatibility: Dogs not permitted

Land status: Nature Conservancy

Fees and permits: None. Refer to www.nature.org/wherewework/ northamerica/states/virginia/preserves/art4948.html for the Nature Conservancy's visitor guidelines.

Schedule: Daily dawn to dusk

Facilities: No facilities and limited parking

Maps: DeLorme *Virginia Atlas & Gazetteer:* Page 75 B6. USGS 7.5 minute series: *Marshall, VA.* See also National Geographic's TOPO! software, Mid-Atlantic Region, Disc 3: Shenandoah.

Trail contacts: Nature Conservancy State Office, Charlottesville, VA; (434) 295-6106; www.nature .org

Finding the trailhead:

Distance from Washington, D.C.: 53 miles

From I-66: Take exit 28. Turn onto US 17 South toward Warrenton. In 0.1 mile, turn right on VA 691 / Carter Run Road. Follow this for 5 miles and turn left on England Mountain Road. In 0.1 mile, turn into the gravel lot on the right that is marked by a trail sign. Trailhead GPS: N38 47.516' / W77 51.342'

THE HIKE

The land that makes up the Wildcat Mountain Natural Area in rural Fauquier County tells two stories. The first is found at a stone wall that marks the top of a steep climb from the parking area. It harkens back to when this area was farmed. Near the northern extent of the hike, on John Trail and Wendy Trail, there are waist-high stone fences. A section is cut out here that lowers the wall's clearance for horses.

The second story is found around Black Cotton Branch and its tributaries. In a sense, this small stream is the centerpiece of a daylong hike through the preserve. All trails descend to the creek banks, or one of its several forks. Thereafter, they climb to heights of 1,000 feet with views that stretch west to the Blue Ridge. Like the views, Black Cotton Branch goes west, flowing from a crease created by four

The Smith house

small mountains—England, Rappahannock, Wildcat, and an unnamed high point at the northern edge of the preserve—to empty into Carter Run, a small tributary of the Rappahannock River.

The farm-to-forest succession of the woodland, coupled with vegetation-rich stream valleys, creates an intriguing mosaic. There are only a few old-growth trees here—the large tulip poplar that marks a junction 1.3 miles into this loop is an exception. Rather, the forest canopy is typical of a pioneering deciduous forest. There are young tulip trees, sweetgum, red maple, and ash. The ash trees seem named for a box of crayons; there are black, red, green, and white ash. White is most typical of the Piedmont forest found on Wildcat Mountain and can be found in that intermediate zone between dry higher elevations and wet lower elevations closer to streams. As Donald Culross Peattie writes in his *Natural History of Trees:* "Every American boy knows a great deal about White Ash wood . . . For it is from White Ash, and White Ash only, that good baseball bats are made."

KID APPEAL

The first 0.5 mile of this hike is a nonstop uphill odyssey—especially if you're knee-high. Consider, after crossing the stone wall at 0.5 mile, going right and making this a modified loop. Take a side jaunt to the Smith House, where, as a reward, kids can play around the pond and the springhouse.

Daffodils growing around old homesite

Humans' imprint on the land is shown again at the Smith House, an abandoned house next to a farm pond. Homesteads that existed on this preserve's land were abandoned after the Civil War. For a period the land was used as an apple farm. A pond like this would have provided a steady year-round source of water to supply the farming activity. In springtime, a choir of frog and toad calls erupt from the heavy vegetation that surrounds the pond. Alone, a spring peeper's song is a single repetitive whistle. More often than not, however, they're heard in large numbers that sound like the jingling of small, delicate bells. The American toad emits a high-pitched trill that can last up to ten seconds long. More startling is the Fowler's toad, which lets loose with a sudden short scream; with some imagination, it sounds just like a mad duck.

Natural plant and tree succession, the history of old farmsteads, the variety of frog calls, and the beauty of a small stream—taken together, there is much to appreciate within the Wildcat Mountain Natural Area.

MILES AND DIRECTIONS

0.0 START from the Wildcat Mountain Trail parking lot on England Mountain Road off VA 691/Carter Run Road. Walk uphill, following a gravel driveway. In 200 steps, where it bends left, turn right (south) onto a dirt road and pass a chain that blocks vehicle traffic, following yellow arrow trail markers.

0.15 Turn left (east) off the dirt road onto a dirt footpath and begin climbing. The route follows thirteen switchbacks as it gains nearly 400 feet over the next 0.5 mile.

0.5 Cross a knee-high stone wall and turn left (north).

1.0 Turn right (east) on a dirt forest road. (**Note:** Left [north] on this road leads to a gate and the boundary of the natural area.)

1.3 Continue straight at a triangle-shaped junction—a wide open space with a huge tree in the middle. (**Note:** The trail that merges on the left is the return portion of this route.)

1.4 Reach a T junction with another forest road and turn left (east).

1.6 Climb to the level of a farm pond and cross on an earthen berm. The Smith House is set on a hillside on your right. At a four-way trail junction in front of the house, arch left and follow a grassy road that descends gently to cross a small seasonal stream. (**Note:** Avoid the trail on your left that cuts back and descends sharply to the springhouse. Also, avoid the grassy road that arcs right and uphill leading to the boundary of the natural area.)

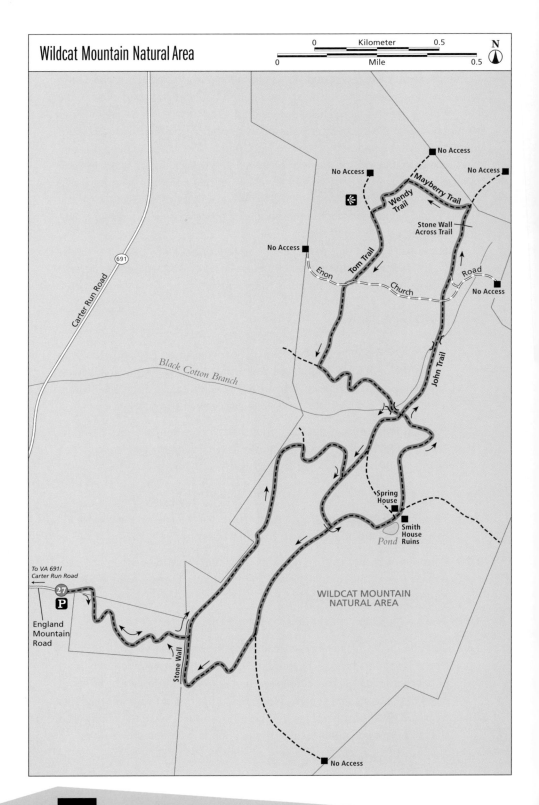

Wildcat Mountain Natural Area

0   Kilometer   0.5

0   Mile   0.5

N

Carter Run Road

691

Black Cotton Branch

No Access

No Access

Mayberry Trail

Wendy Trail

Stone Wall Across Trail

No Access

Tom Trail

Enon

Church

Road

No Access

John Trail

Spring House

Smith House Ruins

Pond

To VA 691/
Carter Run Road

27

P

England Mountain Road

Stone Wall

WILDCAT MOUNTAIN
NATURAL AREA

No Access

1.9 Turn left (west) and continue descending on a woodland path, avoiding the dirt road that stays straight and climbs to the natural area boundary.

1.95 Bear right (north) on John Trail as it climbs up a small stream valley. (**Bail-out:** Turn left [south] at this junction, then left again at an immediate fork in the trail. Resume mileage cues below at 3.6 miles for a 3.5-mile round-trip.)

2.3 Stay straight (north) at a four-way junction with Enon Church Road.

2.4 Skirt a stone wall (or scale it via a low cutout intended for horse passage).

2.5 Turn left (west) on the Mayberry Trail.

2.7 Turn left (south) at an unmarked junction with Wendy Trail.

2.9 Veer right at another stone wall that blocks the path. Wind around the end of the wall and reach a junction with Tom Trail. Bear left (south) and descend on the dirt road trail.

3.0 Turn right (west) on Enon Church Road. Ahead, in less than 0.1 mile, turn left (south) on an unmarked trail. (**FYI:** Use a large boulder on the left at this junction as a landmark.)

3.3 Turn left (east) on another dirt forest road.

3.6 Descend and cross Black Cotton Branch. Climb the opposite bank and veer right (south) on a footpath. (**Note:** The junction uphill on your left is John Trail.)

3.7 Turn right (west), cross a small stream, and climb.

3.8 Stay to the left (south) at a triangle-shaped junction. (**FYI:** This junction is the same one passed at 1.3 miles.)

3.9 Turn right (south) and begin climbing on a wide forest road.

4.3 Veer right (west) off the dirt road and begin a scenic walk across the top of a knoll on a woodland footpath. Ahead, the trail will swing hard right (north) to follow a knee-high stone wall.

4.6 After tracing a stone wall for 0.1 mile, turn left (west) in a gap in the stone wall. Descend to the trailhead parking lot.

5.1 HIKE ENDS at the trailhead parking lot.

HIKE INFORMATION

Local information: Warrenton-Fauquier Visitor's Center, 33 N. Calhoun St., Warrenton, VA; (800) 820-1021; www. visitfauquier.com. Provides information on area wineries, B&Bs, dining, and museums.

Good eats: The Natural Marketplace, 5 Diagonal St., Warrenton, VA; (540) 349-4111; www.thenaturalmarketplace.com. Order from the organic take-out deli and juice bar. You can even arrange for a therapeutic massage after your hike!

Local outdoor stores: Blue Ridge Mountain Sports, 251 W. Lee Hwy., Warrenton, VA; (540) 428-3136; www.brms.com

Organizations: The Nature Conservancy, Charlottesville, VA; (434) 295-6106; www.nature.org/wherewework/northamerica/states/virginia/contact/

🐿️ **Green Tip:**
Be courteous of others. Many people visit natural areas for quiet, peace, and solitude, so avoid making loud noises and intruding on others' privacy.

District of Columbia

Biking past Peirce's Mill

Washington, D.C., hiking excursions can be divided into three broad categories: urban, stream valley, and public gardens. As our featured hikes show, when you can mix all three into select hikes, a special experience awaits.

And what a city! Pierre L'Enfant designed it in 1791 with an eye toward creating a new Rome, a beacon of freedom for the world. Yet the nation's capital remained a stagnant tidal backwater until massive public works campaigns of the late 1800s, and a visionary Beaux-Arts policy outlined by the McMillan Commission in 1902, laid the groundwork for the modern-day city. And when we say "laid the groundwork," we mean it literally. When you walk along West Potomac Park, you're stepping on filled land that was once a stagnant swampy backwater of the Potomac River, subject to tidal flooding.

Rock Creek Park is Washington's recreation epicenter, and rightly so. Advocates campaigned for its creation for more than twenty years, starting in the

1860s, before they ever saw their vision realized. It is the most rugged and expansive example of a peculiar D.C. outdoor recreation outlet: the stream valley park. So it is that a hiker can follow Foundry Branch and Battery Kemble Run, city streets, manicured gardens, and the C&O Canal National Historic Trail for an urban hike that is guaranteed to reshape your image of the city. It is ironic that the stream valley parks, oases of greenery, survived largely through indifference and were long abused by pollution. They now harbor some of the city's last vestiges of un-manicured natural beauty and diversity.

Even the National Mall, that great public space marked by larger and ever larger monuments to people and events in our history, is largely green space. Under the tall old oak trees that shade the World War I memorial, it is possible to re-imagine Washington not as an urban core, but as one great big outdoor playground.

Paddle boats on the tidal basin

Georgetown Loop (Rock Creek Park South)

Washington's stream valley parks are a world apart from the city streets that are within earshot throughout this 12-mile hike. The trails follow small brooks through centuries-old forests in a world where seeing a fox scoot across the trail is not unusual. It's a world well known to dog walkers and runners, but it's lesser known to hikers and naturalists. With that in mind, this route links ten different trails and city sidewalks for a full-day trek for the ambitious hiker. The route skirts community gardens, passes through old Georgetown neighborhoods, and crests near one of the highest points in the city.

Start: From Peirce Mill on Tilden Street

Distance: 12.3-mile loop

Approximate hiking time: 4 to 5 hours

Difficulty: Moderate due to length and numerous road crossings

Trail surface: Stone path, paved bike path, dirt path, paved city street, stairs, footbridge, tunnel, streambed, street crossings, stream crossings

Seasons: Summer

Other trail users: Some portions of this route are used by joggers, walkers, in-line skaters, bicyclists, cross-country skiers; other sections are hiker-only

Handicapped accessibility: In general, the paved bike paths are accessible

Canine compatibility: Leashed dogs permitted

Land status: National park

Fees and permits: None

Schedule: The park is open daily during daylight hours. Peirce Barn at the old mill site is open noon to 5:00 p.m. on weekends.

Facilities: Bathrooms and a snack bar at Fletcher's Boat House; restrooms at Picnic Area 1 in Rock Creek Park, adjacent to Peirce Mill

Maps: DeLorme *Maryland/Delaware Atlas & Gazetteer:* Page 46 C3. USGS 7.5 minute series: *Washington West, DC, MD, VA.* Also, the Potomac Appalachian Trail Club's (PATC) *Map N: Rock Creek Park Area.* The map inset details parks and trails used on this hike.

Trail contacts: Rock Creek Park, 3545 Williamsburg Lane NW, Washington, D.C. 20008; (202) 895-6000; www.nps.gov/rocr. PATC (see *Hike Information*) maintains the stream valley trails.

Special considerations: The Rock Creek and Potomac Parkway traffic flow is altered for weekday rush hour traffic. From Connecticut Avenue, it is one-way going south between 6:45 and 9:30 a.m., and one-way going north from 3:45 to 6:30 p.m. Also, access streets like Glover Road, Ross Drive, Bingham Drive, and Sherrill Drive are not maintained after heavy snowfall or in icy conditions.

Canal Road, which separates Battery Kemble Park from Fletcher's Boat House and the C&O Canal National Historic Park, is a significant obstacle on this route. A culvert passes beneath the road and is tall enough for walkers to pass.

However, hikers must have the agility to scale a head-high fence at the far end. Fence slats are sturdy and widely spaced, and climbing it is akin to climbing up a stepladder. We recommend against crossing over Canal Road. There is virtually no road shoulder, and traffic moves past at full speed. The embankment is steep; slipping down into the roadway is a real possibility. If you cannot pass beneath Canal Road via the culvert, skip the lower leg of Battery Kemble Park. Instead, turn left and walk MacArthur Boulevard to Glover-Archibold Park's southern trailhead. Resume the hiking directions at the 6.7-mile cue.

Finding the trailhead:
From Northern Virginia: Cross the Potomac on I-66 / US 50 via the Theodore Roosevelt Memorial Bridge. Take the Independence Avenue exit (right lane). After merging onto Independence, in quick succession turn right and merge onto Rock Creek and Potomac Parkway. In 0.7 mile, continue straight at an intersection with Virginia Avenue. As signs indicate that Connecticut Avenue is approaching, stay right and follow signs for the National Zoo and Beach Drive. (*Note:* The Rock Creek and Potomac Parkway ends at Connecticut Avenue; Beach Drive becomes the main north–south route through Rock Creek Park.) Continue straight on Beach Drive, with Klingle Avenue on the left and Piney Branch Parkway on the right. At the four-way stoplight with Beach Road, Park Road (on the right), and Tilden Street (on the left), turn left onto Tilden Street. Cross Rock Creek and turn right into the parking area for Peirce Mill.
From downtown Washington, D.C.: Follow directions above from the intersection of the Rock Creek and Potomac Parkway and Virginia Avenue. Or, follow Connecticut Avenue northwest from DuPont Circle for 2.3 miles and turn right on Tilden Street. In another 0.5 mile, turn left into Peirce Mill parking area.
From Maryland and I-495 (Capital Beltway): Take exit 33 (Connecticut Avenue, Chevy Chase, Kensington) and follow it south toward Chevy Chase. In

4.6 miles, turn right on Tilden Street. In another 0.5 mile, turn left into Peirce Mill parking area.

Public transportation: The Red Line offers three stops in proximity to this route. The closest are Cleveland Park and UDC–Van Ness. From either you can pick up the Melvin Hazen Trail where it crosses Connecticut Avenue (start Miles and Directions at 0.7 mile from the trailhead). Tenleytown–UA Metro is closer to Glover-Archibold Park. See Options below for a revised route if you use this Metro station. Trailhead GPS: N38 56.418' / W77 03.117'

THE HIKE

In a city of monuments and imposing edifices, Washington's stream valley parks persist as small oases of nature. Tree-shaded corridors form a loop around Georgetown, where inconspicuous streams pass through city neighborhoods en route to the Potomac River and Rock Creek. The forests shading them are much loved by their neighbors as running paths, community gardens, and dog-walking routes. Mature stands of tulip poplar, beech, and sycamore trees provide shelter for the urban wildlife quartet: raccoon, fox, opossum, and deer. Understory shrubs—many others exotic and invasive (and running riot)—attract songbirds that feast on the berry-producing plants.

The stream valley parks that surround Georgetown present the best opportunity to link many disparate parks and trails into a single route. It begins with Rock Creek Park, the granddaddy of them all. The Parkway Trail along Rock Creek,

Urban Hiking

Within the first mile into this route, hikers will confront the busy, four-lane-wide Connecticut Avenue. As the crow flies, the route continues straight across the street. But as city law dictates, our described route turns right (north) to the nearest traffic light and crosswalk. D.C. traffic laws state: "Between adjacent intersections controlled by traffic control signal devices or by police officers, pedestrians shall not cross the roadway at any place except in a crosswalk." And so it is with all of our city walking directions: Where there is an option between the shortcut or the law, we chose the law. Not every road crossing on this route is controlled by signal devices or other means. In these instances, traffic laws dictate that pedestrians outside a crosswalk must yield the right-of-way to vehicles, and they should cross at right angles to the sidewalk. Learn more about laws related to pedestrians and traffic laws at http://dmv.dc.gov/info/DMV Municipal Regulations.shtm.

Glover-Archibold Trail along Foundry Branch, and Battery Kemble Trail along its namesake stream are the three pillars. These are north-to-south routes that follow streams winding through city neighborhoods to meet the slack waters of the Potomac beneath Georgetown Heights.

Linking them are small east–west connectors: the Melvin Hazen Trail, the Wesley Heights Trail, the Chesapeake and Ohio National Historic Trail, the Whitehaven Trail, and the Dumbarton Oaks Trail. These routes cross the grain of terrain. They're hilly and winding, where the stream valley trails are straight and descending. It is on these routes that you'll get your exercise as you climb out of one valley and descend into the next.

Exhibit A for how unpredictable this walk will be: Within the first 0.5 mile, you will start the hike at Peirce Mill in Rock Creek Park, a gristmill and one of the earliest industries of the Washington, D.C., area. Pass through open fields at Picnic Area 1. Enter the woods along Melvin Hazen Branch, the first stream valley park of this route. (It's a beauty: narrow, steep, and windy.) Follow a trail that rock-hops the stream and, after the last picture-perfect wading pool, climb up the stream slope. Skirt the back wall of an apartment building and emerge onto Connecticut Avenue. In quick order, navigate four lanes of zip-zip-zip traffic and walk up Rod-

These urban trails cross roadways.

man Street and its row of tidy single-family homes. Where the sidewalk ends, keep walking, and there, on the right, spy a wood sign with yellow words. (Here, when we took this hike, we re-entered the cool shade of the wood and watched, mouths agape, as a fox coolly padded downhill to the stream. Our exclamations startled the small canine, and it scooted out of sight. For the next 0.5 mile, until the trail rose once more out of wooded stream valley to another city street, this flash of wildlife consumed our imagination.)

The city's stream valley parks hold moments of beauty. As the days lengthen and temperatures rise, spring beauty and cut-leaved toothwort will poke up through the leaf litter of the forest floors. Six or seven months later, in autumn, tulip poplar leaves turn yellow, and maple leaves turn red. In late winter, the American beech tree still clings to its paper-thin leaves that sound like a gentle maraca when the wind rustles the branches.

It wasn't always this pretty. Washington's stream valley parks are holdovers from an era when a creek, any creek, was a city sewer. The raw waste dumped into them was swept away downstream. Smelly and foul, a potential source of disease and generally unpleasant, they were largely ignored. From this abuse, unintended consequences—unforeseen, you might argue—arose. As woodlands were cleared to accommodate a growing Washington and Georgetown community, trees in the stream valleys were spared. As hikers, we can enjoy the results.

MILES AND DIRECTIONS

0.0 START at Peirce Mill, a colonial-era gristmill. Follow a stone path down past the mill to a bike path that parallels the stream. Turn right (south) on the bike path, which is Western Ridge Trail. Pass beneath a bridge and walk past Picnic Area 1 on the right. Where the bike path crosses Rock Creek on a pedestrian bridge, turn right (west) and walk across a grass field to the edge of the forest.

0.2 Enter the woods on the Melvin Hazen Trail, a dirt footpath marked by a yellow blaze on a wooden post. (**Note:** Western Ridge Trail heads left [south] from this junction and is the return portion of this hike.)

Glover-Archibold Park is named for two icons of Washington, D.C., society, Charles Carroll Glover and Anne Archibold. Charles Carroll Glover was a banker and philanthropist better known for spearheading the creation of Rock Creek Park and construction of the National Cathedral in the late 1800s. Anne Archibold was a Standard Oil heiress who bequeathed the land for public use.

Georgetown Loop (Rock Creek Park South)

0.7 Exit the woods onto Connecticut Avenue. Cross the street at a traffic light to the right, then double back on Connecticut as far as Rodman Street NW. Turn right (west) on Rodman and walk up the residential street.

0.9 Beyond where the sidewalk ends on Rodman Street, look right for a wooden sign marking the Melvin Hazen Trail. Reenter the woods here and immediately turn left at a T junction to descend to the stream on a single-track dirt path.

1.3 Emerge from the woods at Reno Road and Tilden Street NW. Turn left, cross Reno Road, and walk up Springland Lane.

1.5 Springland Lane ends in a cul-de-sac. Find a stone-laid path at the back of the paved circle and follow it up a small set of stairs. Turn right on a wide grass easement. This strip empties onto Idaho Avenue NW, a short residential street. Where Idaho ends, turn left onto Tilden Street. At Tilden and 37th Street, turn right and walk 2 blocks to Van Ness Street (crossing over Upton Street en route).

1.8 Turn left (west) on Van Ness Street.

2.0 Cross Wisconsin Avenue and walk downhill. In 0.1 mile, turn left onto a well-worn dirt path and cross a grassy field. There is a sign at this junction for Glover-Archibold Park. At the far end of the field, the park enters the woods and descends into the Foundry Branch stream valley.

2.7 Emerge from the woods and follow the dirt path across a grass field to Massachusetts Avenue. Cross diagonally right and reenter woods on the opposite side. The trail descends as a dirt footpath.

3.2 Cross Cathedral Avenue. Drop off the roadside on a set of stairs with hand-rails.

3.3 Cross New Mexico Avenue diagonally left at the intersection with Garfield Street. Descend back into the stream valley park on wide steps. When the trail levels, cross a footbridge.

3.5 Stay straight at a junction with a trail that intersects on the right.

3.7 Turn right (west) onto the Wesley Heights Trail. Cross Foundry Branch on stream rocks. The trail follows a small tributary of Foundry Branch as it climbs.

3.8 Cross the stream and climb the embankment to a T junction. Turn right and continue on the Wesley Heights Trail.

3.9 Exit the woods onto 44th Street, cross, and turn right (north) on the side-walk. Walk 200 feet and turn left to descend a short flight of stairs. The trail thereafter is a dirt footpath. (**Note:** Trail markings here are scant; avoid an unmarked footpath that enters the woods directly opposite where you exit onto 44th Street.)

KID APPEAL

The restored Peirce Mill in Rock Creek Park demonstrates how colonial-era millers ground wheat into flour. The mill's wooden parts are restored, and there's a millstone powered from a stream. Next door in Peirce Barn, kids can try on old-fashioned clothes and play with nineteenth-century toys.

4.1 Cross Foxhall Road and reenter to descend into the woods at a wooden trail sign and a National Park Service boundary stick.

4.4 Cross 49th Street diagonally left and enter Battery Kemble Park. A lone yellow blaze on a tree marks the trailhead here, but the dirt trail is wide and self-evident. Descend to Battery Kemble Run, cross on a footbridge with railings, and climb the stream embankment to a T junction. Turn left (south) and follow a dirt footpath.

4.8 Cross MacArthur Boulevard to the Conduit Road Schoolhouse, a red building. Re-enter the woods on a dirt path to the left of this building. (**Note:** Built in 1864 and operational until the 1920s, the schoolhouse is on the National Register of Historic Places and presently houses the Discovery Creek Children's Museum of Washington.)

5.0 Rock-hop Battery Kemble Run to where it passes beneath Canal Road via a culvert. Where it emerges on the other side of the road, climb over a wooden barrier fence and enter Fletcher's Boat House in C&O Canal National Historic Park. Cross the C&O Canal on a footbridge. Turn left (east) onto the canal towpath. (**FYI:** There is a concession stand that sells hot dogs and drinks at Fletcher's Boat House.)

6.7 Descend off the towpath via a long flight of stairs, turn right, and pass beneath the canal via a pedestrian tunnel. Follow the paved path around and up to Canal Road. At the sidewalk, turn right, cross a bridge, and then turn right again onto a dirt path etched into a grass field. This is the southern end of Glover-Archibold Park. Within a few hundred yards, the trail passes beneath an old trestle and enters the woods.

7.2 Climb through an open field to Reservoir Road at 44th Street. Cross Reservoir Road and reenter the park. The dirt footpath descends and follows Foundry Branch.

7.6 Turn right onto Whitehaven Trail.

7.8 Veer left at a fork in the trail. In the next 0.1 mile, turn left and avoid an unmarked, but well-traveled, path that splits right.

8.0 Enter a field after passing a fenced-in community garden. Cross the field diagonally right and, at the far end, beyond a water fountain, reenter the woods. Immediately after, watch for a trail that enters from the right, and pass straight through a four-way trail intersection.

8.2 Enter a small park and follow a well-worn footpath to the sidewalk on 37th Street. Cross the road, keeping a Metro bus shelter to your right. Reenter the woods between Whitehaven on the right and U Street on the left. Pass beneath a residential power line easement and climb a long set of stairs up a steep hillside. (*Stay alert:* The 0.2 mile of trail between 37th Street to Wisconsin Avenue is not well marked. At the top of the steps, avoid an unmarked left-branching trail. A few feet past this, turn left at an unmarked trail junction. Only after this turn are the yellow trail blazes visible. If you miss this turn, the trail drops steeply down to Whitehaven Parkway.)

8.4 Cross 35th Street, pass through a field, and cross Wisconsin Avenue. Walk down Whitehaven Street and, at the base of this dead-end street, look diagonally right across the street for a wooden sign that marks the entrance to Dumbarton Oaks Park.

8.6 Enter Dumbarton Oaks Park on a yellow-blazed dirt footpath.

Exotic non-native species cloak trees along Glover-Archibold Trail.

8.7 Stay straight at a junction with the Normanstone Trail.

8.8 At a fork in the trail, veer right and cross a stream on two wooden planks. The trail from here features masonry walls, stone benches, and small alcoves. The stream, too, has its banks lined with stone.

9.0 Pass out of Dumbarton Oaks Park onto a paved road. Swing left and downhill, cross the road, and reenter the woods on the opposite side on a wide dirt road. As you descend through the woods, the stream is on your left side.

9.1 Cross the stream on a wood footbridge with railings. Descend to Rock Creek and swing left (north) to follow the stream valley on the Parkway Trail, which is a narrow dirt footpath.

9.3 Pass beneath the massive bridge that carries Massachusetts Avenue across Rock Creek.

9.5 Continue straight past the Normanstone Trail.

9.7 Exit the dirt path onto a paved bike trail. Turn left (north) and follow the paved walkway, which is used by joggers, walkers, in-line skaters, and bikers.

10.0 Cross a ramp road that rises left to Connecticut Avenue. Past here, the path crosses beneath Taft Bridge, which carries Connecticut Avenue over Rock Creek.

10.2 Turn left just before Rock Creek Parkway enters a tunnel. Pass through a gate marking the entrance to the National Zoo. (**Note:** From May through August, this gate is open from 6:00 a.m. to 8:00 p.m. From September through April, the gate is open 6:00 a.m. to 6:00 p.m. It is closed on Christmas.)

Dumbarton Oaks

You've descended through stream valleys, crossed roads, and passed through culverts, but the landscaped trail through Dumbarton Oaks is something altogether different. Here, stone benches line little nooks etched into the hillside. The streambed is channeled with precise masonry work. All of it is the legacy of Mildred and Robert Bliss, he a career diplomat, she a garden aficionado. They developed the Dumbarton Oaks property after buying it in the 1920s. Today their estate is divided between the National Park Service and a Harvard University research center for the study of gardens and the history of landscape architecture. More than twenty gardens on the property are open for public enjoyment.

11.8 Veer left off the paved bike path onto Western Ridge Trail, which follows the streamside as a dirt path. The route is blazed green. Within 0.1 mile of this split, Western Ridge splits into a "strenuous" or "moderate" route. A trail sign indicates each route. Choose either.

12.0 Exit the woods in the grass field of Picnic Area 1. Turn right and walk across grass to the paved bike path. Turn left (north) on the path (avoiding the bridge that carries the bike path south across Rock Creek).

12.3 HIKE ENDS at Peirce Mill.

OPTIONS

The Red Line stop at Tenleytown–AU Metro lands you on Wisconsin Avenue. Walk south to the intersection with Tilden Avenue, turn right, and walk down Tilden 0.1 mile to the north entrance to Glover-Archibold Park. (Pick up *Miles and Directions* at mile 2.0.) If you choose this start option, you can shorten the loop by eliminating Whitehaven Parkway, Dumbarton Oaks, and the West Ridge Trail. After turning north from the C&O Canal National Historic Trail onto Glover-Archibold Trail, stay straight on G-A Trail until you return to Tilden Avenue. Retrace your steps to the Tenleytown–AU Metro.

HIKE INFORMATION

Local information: Destination DC, Washington, D.C.; (202) 789-7000; www.washington.org

Local events/attractions: The National Zoo, 3001 Connecticut Ave. NW, Washington, D.C.; (202) 633-4800; http://nationalzoo.si.edu. The nation's zoo is adjacent to the hike and is part of the Smithsonian Institution.

Good eats: The National Zoo has several cafes and snack carts where you can get hamburgers, salads, pizza, and subs

Local outdoor stores: Hudson Trail Outfitters, 4530 Wisconsin Ave. NW, Washington, D.C.; (202) 363-9810; www.hudsontrail.com

Hike tours: Rock Creek Park rangers lead programs throughout the year

Organizations: Potomac Appalachian Trail Club (PATC), 118 Park St. SE, Vienna, VA; (703) 242-0315; www.potomacappalachian.org. Maintains many of the trails and produces a map.

> *The name Dumbarton dates back to the original land patent of 1703 in what is today Georgetown, given to Ninian Beall, a Scotsman. He named the high rock promontory for Dumbarton Rock in his homeland.*

National Mall Monuments

Nearly 2 miles in length, anchored by memorials from end to end, the National Mall today embodies the spirit, if not the exact design, of Pierre-Charles L'Enfant's original vision for Washington, D.C.: a grand lawn and boulevard that is both a gathering place and a symbol of American democracy. There are as many ways to explore the Mall as there are visitors. Our route, from first footsteps to last, traces the evolution of "America's front lawn" from yesteryear's dirt roads and open canals to today's green space and iconic monuments. By trip's end, you'll have visited thirteen memorials and monuments—a monumental feat unto itself.

Start: From the Tidal Basin Inlet bridge on Ohio Drive SW. *Alternate start:* If arriving on the Mall via Metro, start at the Washington Monument ticket office on 15th Street NW.

Distance: 4.6-mile loop, with an option of adding a 4.3-mile loop through East Potomac Park

Approximate hiking time: 2 hours for each loop

Difficulty: Easy due to paved paths, no elevation gain, and services like snack bars, bathrooms, park benches, and water fountains

Trail surface: Paved footpaths and roads

Seasons: May through Nov. Expect larger than normal crowds on weekends, and in May when the cherry blossoms bloom.

Other trail users: Pedestrians, joggers, bike riders, tourists

Handicapped accessibility: Most of the Mall is handicapped accessible. The Big Three memorials—Jefferson, Washington, and Lincoln—have elevators.

Canine compatibility: Leashed dogs are allowed on the National Mall, but not inside specific monuments or memorials. The lone exception is the Franklin Delano Roosevelt Memorial. Dogs are not allowed on the walkways through the Vietnam Veterans, World War II, or Korean War Veterans National Memorial.

Land status: National park

Fees and permits: None

Schedule: 24 hours a day

Facilities: The Jefferson, Washington, and Lincoln Memorials have public restrooms, visitor centers, and gift shops. The official visitor center for the entire National Mall & Memorial Park is located on 17th Avenue near the intersection with Independence.

Maps: DeLorme *Maryland/Delaware Atlas & Gazetteer:* Page 46 D3. USGS 7.5 minute series: *Washington West, DC, MD, VA.* National Park Service map of the downtown Mall is available at the park visitor center or any information booth

at the Jefferson and Washington Memorials.
Trail contacts: National Mall & Memorial Parks, 900 Ohio Dr. SW, Washington, D.C. 20024; (202) 426-6841; www.nps.gov/nama
Special considerations: Free tickets to visit inside the Washington Monument are available starting 8:30 a.m. on the morning of your visit, on a first-come, first-served basis. Individuals may reserve tickets ahead of time by calling (877) 444-6777 or visiting www.recreation.gov.

Finding the trailhead:
From I-395 (Virginia): Drive north on combined I-395/US 1 across the Potomac River. Bear right to stay on I-395 where the highways split and US 1 goes straight. Take the next exit, on the right, for Potomac Park and Park Police (commercial trucks are prohibited). At the bottom of the ramp, turn right on Buckeye Drive SW. In 0.1 mile, turn right on Ohio Drive SW. Park in any one of the large parking lots on the right in the next 0.3 mile. After parking, walk north on a paved footpath along the Potomac River. Reach the trailhead, at the Tidal Basin Inlet bridge, in 0.2 mile.
Alternate parking: If the parking lots are full, continue straight (north) on Ohio Drive SW. Cross the Tidal Basin Inlet. The section of Ohio Drive SW between the Tidal Basin and Independence Drive SW features on-street parking. After parking, walk south on a paved path along the Potomac to reach the trailhead at the Tidal Basin Inlet bridge.
Public transportation: Orange and Blue Lines have service to Smithsonian Station. Exit the station onto the National Mall, turn south, and walk toward the Washington Monument. Begin *Miles and Directions* from the Washington Monument. Trailhead GPS: Tidal Basin Inlet: N38 52.808' / W77 02.420'; Washington Monument: N38 53.364' / W77 01.993'

THE HIKE

Electric describes the scene as you explore the National Mall. Throngs move in seemingly all directions. Kites swoop, soar, and swoop again overhead. On huge open lawns, kids kick a soccer ball. Bike riders and joggers weave in between people whose eyes are cast upward, soaking in monuments and memorials. The Mall is big enough to accommodate this activity—and much more. Yet if explored thoroughly, it turns out to be a place dotted with small curiosities and quiet, tucked-away spots that make it feel personal and intimate.

Like moths drawn to the light, our footsteps carry us to the base of the Washington Monument. This is not just the defining architecture of the Mall, but of all Washington. Whether from the heights of Georgetown or the Potomac River's edge in Virginia, it dominates the skyline. That's no accident. City ordinances dictate that no building can be built to exceed the monument's 555-foot height.

The story of its construction could occupy a television miniseries. Pierre L'Enfant, the French engineer who designed the capital city in 1791, envisioned a monument to Washington as part of his "monument core." His idea of a bronze sculpture—Washington on a horse—gave way to the obelisk. From afar, you might notice the stone is two different shades, lighter below and darker on top. It's about 150 feet up from the ground and marks the spot where construction stopped for twenty years, from 1858 to 1878 (including the Civil War years). When construction resumed, the quarry stone could not be matched, resulting in the different shades.

Walking around the base of the Washington Monument, we experienced a sense of vertigo as we looked skyward, and it seemed as if it was leaning, leaning . . . leaning. Forcing our eyes toward the ground, we spotted a small piece of square granite sticking out of the ground. A sign on this 2-foot-by-2-foot stone identified it as Jefferson Pier. If, in looking around, you wonder why a docking pier was located in this landlocked spot, you're not alone.

When we did research about the National Mall later, it became the thread that unraveled the long history of the National Mall and its evolution.

World War II Memorial

Tiber is a name that harkens back to the Tiber River in Italy, and Rome, the city that was built on its banks. Tiber Creek, the small tributary that flowed through Washington, D.C., was called Goose Creek in colonial times, but Tiber better captured the grandeur L'Enfant envisioned for America's capital city—the new Rome.

Jefferson Pier once stood on the banks of Tiber Creek, a small tributary that flowed south past Capitol Hill and emptied into the Potomac in an area known as Potomac Flats (or, as one congressman once declared, a "damn swamp"). If, in the mid-1800s, you stood at the pier and looked west, you would be looking out over a swamp that was part of the tidal Potomac. The creek soon became a canal, and for a time it served as an open sewer. The roads around it were dirt and the homes shanties and shacks. Starting in 1872, under an ambitious public works program, the canal was enclosed in concrete (its route today is approximated by Constitution Avenue). Then, in 1882, the U.S. Army Corps of Engineers began filling in Potomac Flats. The swampland turned into land that would later become West Potomac Park.

The pier itself? Although it was on the banks of a navigable creek, it was not meant as a boat tie-up. Rather, Jefferson ordered it installed to mark a Prime Meridian for the new United States. It marks the spot where a line drawn due south from the White House intersects with a line drawn due west from the U.S. Capitol. This was mile marker zero, the point from which miles east and, more significantly, west were measured. (The Prime Meridian now is in Greenwich, England.)

It is somehow fitting for a hike that celebrates men and women, their contributions and sacrifices, to be entirely on man-made ground (this including the optional East Potomac Park leg down to Hains Point). The latest grand monument to be erected here is the World War II Memorial. Set at the east end of the Reflecting

The Two Halves of the National Mall

The National Mall, 2 miles in length, is anchored on the east end by the U.S. Capitol and on the west by the Lincoln Memorial. Halfway between is the Washington Monument. Bounding it to the north is the White House, and to the south, the Jefferson Memorial. It's easily divided into two parts. The eastern half from the Capitol to the Washington Monument is Museum Row, where more than ten museums line the Mall, including the Smithsonian Institute. The bulk of this hike takes place in the western half of the Mall, the monument core, more formally known as West Potomac Park. The long, skinny Reflecting Pool is the centerpiece; around it stand all the well-known memorials, from the oldest (Washington) to the newest (the World War II Memorial).

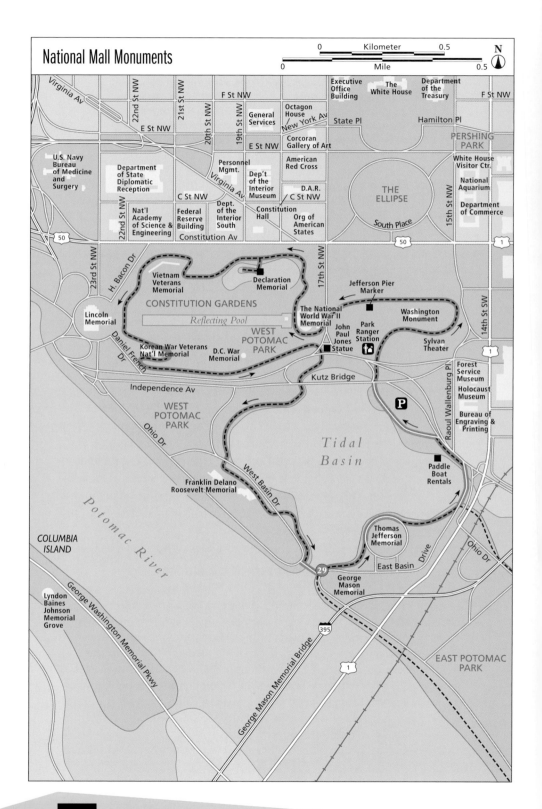

National Mall Monuments

Kilometer
0   0.5

Mile
0   0.5

N

Virginia Av
22nd St NW
21st St NW
20th St NW
19th St NW
F St NW
Executive Office Building
The White House
Department of the Treasury
F St NW

E St NW
General Services
Octagon House
New York Av
State Pl
Hamilton Pl
PERSHING PARK

E St NW
Personnel Mgmt.
Corcoran Gallery of Art

U.S. Navy Bureau of Medicine and Surgery
Department of State Diplomatic Reception
Virginia Av
Dep't of the Interior Museum
American Red Cross
THE ELLIPSE
White House Visitor Ctr.
National Aquarium

C St NW
D.A.R.
C St NW
Department of Commerce

22nd St NW
Nat'l Academy of Science & Engineering
Federal Reserve Building
Dept. of the Interior South
Constitution Hall
Org of American States
South Place
15th St NW
14th St SW

Constitution Av
50
50
1

23rd St NW
H. Bacon Dr
Vietnam Veterans Memorial
Declaration Memorial
Jefferson Pier Marker

CONSTITUTION GARDENS
17th St NW

Lincoln Memorial
Reflecting Pool
The National World War II Memorial
Washington Monument

Daniel French Dr
WEST POTOMAC PARK
John Paul Jones Statue
Park Ranger Station
Sylvan Theater

Korean War Veterans Nat'l Memorial
D.C. War Memorial
Kutz Bridge
Forest Service Museum

Independence Av
Raoul Wallenberg Pl
Holocaust Museum

WEST POTOMAC PARK
Ohio Dr
P
Bureau of Engraving & Printing

Tidal Basin

West Basin Dr
Paddle Boat Rentals

Franklin Delano Roosevelt Memorial

Potomac River

COLUMBIA ISLAND
Thomas Jefferson Memorial
East Basin
Ohio Dr

29
George Mason Memorial

Lyndon Baines Johnson Memorial Grove
George Washington Memorial Pkwy
George Mason Memorial Bridge
395
1
EAST POTOMAC PARK

Pool, the memorial is all white marble, dramatic sculptures, and powerfully wrought inscriptions of patriotism, sacrifice, and duty set amid pools and fountains. A different sort of inspiration awaits in nearby Constitution Gardens, a tree-shaded oasis on the north side of the Reflecting Pool. This memorial, grassy and passive, has a small pool and an island reached via a footbridge. Here, big willow trees droop long wavy branches over a modest display honoring the fifty-six signers of the Declaration of Independence. Canada geese cruise the pond waters near to shore.

If, after hitting the Vietnam Veterans, Lincoln, and Korean War Veterans Memorials—and with the Franklin Delano Roosevelt still to come—you start feeling monument fatigue, follow our footsteps to the D.C. War Memorial. It is on the south side of the Reflecting Pool. A microforest of tall oak trees shades a small rotunda supported by Roman-like columns. It was built in honor of Washington, D.C.'s, World War I veterans, of which 26,000 served. It is set off from both road and sidewalk, and therefore it is less noticeable. As if transported, we walked actual dirt paths through the trees and emerged in the bright sunshine that lighted and warmed the rotunda.

If there was ever a place on the National Mall to read a book beneath a tree, this would be it. And if we could recommend a title, it would be *Spring in Washington* by Louis J. Halle, a natural history of how a city springs to life anew each year.

MILES AND DIRECTIONS

0.0   START from the Tidal Basin Inlet bridge on Ohio Drive SW. At the east end of the bridge, turn right (north) and cross East Basin Drive to enter the George Mason Memorial.

0.1   Recross East Basin Drive SW, walking north, then veer right on a sidewalk that skirts the edge of the Tidal Basin beneath the shade of cherry trees.

0.4   Enter the Jefferson Memorial at the base of a large flight of stairs leading to the rotunda. After exploring, return to the base of these stairs and turn right on the sidewalk that encircles the Tidal Basin. As you circle toward Independence Avenue, pass over the Tidal Basin outlet and a paddleboat concession.

1.0   Cross straight over Independence Avenue and walk past the National Park Service offices for the National Mall and Memorial Garden. (**Note:** This office is not the main visitor center for the park.)

1.2   Turn right (east) and begin a long walk around the base of the Washington Monument.

1.4 Pass the ticket office for the Washington Monument. Continue circling the north side of the monument. Walk straight (west) down the Mall toward the World War II Memorial. Pass the Jefferson Pier marker en route. (**FYI:** There are restrooms in the ticket office building.)

1.8 Cross straight over 17th Street and enter the World War II Memorial. After exploring, exit the memorial on its right (north) side and follow a sidewalk that leads up a gentle slope.

2.0 Enter the Constitution Gardens. Bear right (north) on a path that circles a pond on your left.

2.2 Reach the 56 Signers of the Declaration of Independence Memorial by turning left (south) and crossing a footbridge onto a small island. After exploring, retrace your footsteps over the bridge and turn left (west).

2.6 Enter the Vietnam Veterans Memorial near the Vietnam Women's Memorial. Exit at the west end of the memorial, near the *Three Servicemen* sculpture. Follow Harry Bacon Drive west toward the Lincoln Memorial.

2.9 Reach the base of the Lincoln Memorial. A long flight of stairs leads up to the portico. After exploring, return to this spot, turn right (south), and follow a sidewalk that crosses a road. Your route parallels Daniel French Drive, but you veer left, following signs for the Korean War Veterans Memorial.

3.1 Reach the Korean War Veterans Memorial. After exploring, return to Daniel French Drive and follow a sidewalk left. At an intersection with Independence Avenue, turn left (east) and continue walking.

3.3 Veer left off the sidewalk onto a dirt path.

3.5 Reach the D.C. War Memorial, a circular portico lined with Roman-style arches and shaded by large oak trees. After exploring, exit the memorial by following a sidewalk past the bathrooms.

3.7 Reach the National Mall Visitors Center on 17th Street. Turn right (south) and head toward Independence Avenue.

3.8 In succession, cross the westbound and eastbound lanes of Independence Avenue. (**Note:** That's a statue of John Paul Jones in a traffic island at the junction of 17th Street and Independence Avenue.)

3.9 Turn right on a sidewalk that skirts the Tidal Basin. (**FYI:** On the left you'll find the first Japanese cherry tree given to the United States as a gesture of friendship by the city of Tokyo, in 1912. It grows in a small grove on the right, marked by a small stone.)

4.2 Turn right and climb a staircase into the Franklin Delano Roosevelt Memorial. After exploring, exit the memorial at the east end and resume walking along the Tidal Basin.

4.6 HIKE ENDS at the bridge over the Tidal Basin inlet.

OPTIONS

East Potomac Park is a narrow peninsula that extends southeast along the Potomac River. It's best known for the public golf course and as a bike-riding circuit. You can add another 4.3 miles to your walk by including a loop through the park. Trails are on paved sidewalks, which you'll share with anglers and parents with strollers. Hains Point, at the southern tip, is named for Maj. Peter Conover Hains of the U.S. Army Corps, who oversaw creation of East and West Potomac Parks out of the mudflats of the Potomac River.

HIKE INFORMATION

Local information: Destination DC, Washington, D.C.; (202) 789-7000; www .washington.org

Local events/attractions: The Smithsonian Kite Festival is held annually at the Washington Monument. Morning hours are devoted to kite-making competitions. In the afternoon, kites take to the air for competition flying. Children's activities abound. Details are online at http://kitefestival.org.

Eastern Market, 7th Street and North Carolina Avenue SE, Washington, D.C.; www .easternmarketdc.com. Local merchants offer produce, flowers, baked goods, and meats, inside during the week and in an open-air farmers' market on weekends, year-round.

Good eats: There are refreshment stands outside the monuments where you can get a quick hot dog, or you can have lunch inside one of the Smithsonian museum cafes

Local outdoor stores: City Sports, 715 7th St. NW, Washington, D.C.; (202) 544-6083; www.citysports.com

Hike tours: The park offers ranger-led walking tours, as do many private tour companies. Dates and times for NPS walks and programs are found in the *Mall Times*, a monthly newspaper issued by the National Park Service.

Other resources: *City of Trees: The Complete Field Guide to the Trees of Washington, D.C.,* by Melanie Choukas-Bradley and Polly Alexander

Rock Creek Park North

As far back as 1866, people recognized Rock Creek's natural beauty and fought to protect it. It would be another quarter century before an actual park came into being. Long, narrow, and heavily wooded, this 10-mile-long park is a twisty green stripe through a sea of urbanism. It is also a magnet for hikers, joggers, horseback riders, and others. The spacious northern section of the park is big enough to hold them all. Here, it is hilly and wooded, with room to roam.

Start: From the Rock Creek Nature Center

Distance: 7.1-mile loop

Approximate hiking time: 3 hours

Difficulty: Moderate due to distance and some confusing trail junctions

Trail surface: Paved paths, dirt woodland paths, roads

Seasons: Best in summer

Other trail users: Horseback riders, joggers, walkers, in-line skaters, and bikers

Handicapped accessibility: The Edge of Wood Trail at the nature center is paved and has a rope guide for the visually impaired

Canine compatibility: Leashed dogs permitted

Land status: National park

Fees and permits: No entrance fee or permits, although a fee and permit are required for groups using the picnic area

Schedule: The park is open daily during daylight hours. The nature center is open Wed through Sat 9:00 a.m. to 5:00 p.m. and closed Thanksgiving, Christmas, and New Year's Day.

Facilities: There are restrooms at the nature center and a chemical toilet at the Boundary Bridge parking area. The nature center features natural-history displays and a planetarium. Throughout Rock Creek Park are historic buildings, tennis courts, a golf course, and an equestrian center.

Maps: DeLorme *Maryland/Delaware Atlas & Gazetteer:* Page 46 B3. USGS 7.5 minute series: *Washington West, DC, MD, VA.* Also, the Potomac Appalachian Trail Club's (PATC) *Map N: Rock Creek Park Area.*

Trail contacts: Rock Creek Park, 3545 Williamsburg Lane NW, Washington, D.C. 20008; (202) 895-6000; www.nps.gov/rocr

Special considerations: The park closes sections of Beach Drive to cars from 7:00 a.m. to 7:00 p.m. on weekends and federal holidays for recreational use by hikers, bicyclists, runners, and in-line skaters. Closed sections are: Beach Drive north from Broad Branch Road to Military Road; from Picnic Area 10 to Wise Road; and from

West Beach Drive to the Boundary Bridge parking area. Bingham Drive and Sherrill Drive are also closed to cars on weekends and federal holidays.

In the south region of the park, the Rock Creek and Potomac Parkway traffic flow is altered for weekday rush hour traffic. From Connecticut Avenue it is one-way going south between 6:45 and 9:30 a.m., and one-way going north from 3:45 to 6:30 p.m. Also, access streets like Glover Road, Ross Drive, Bingham Drive, and Sherrill Drive are not maintained after heavy snowfall or in icy conditions.

Finding the trailhead:

From Northern Virginia: Cross the Potomac on I-66/US 50 (the Theodore Roosevelt Memorial Bridge). Take the Independence Avenue exit (right lane) and, after merging onto Independence, in quick succession turn right and merge onto Rock Creek and Potomac Parkway. In 0.7 mile, continue straight at an intersection with Virginia Avenue. As road signs indicate Connecticut Avenue approaching, stay right and follow signs for the National Zoo and Beach Drive. (*Note:* The Rock Creek and Potomac Parkway ends at Connecticut Avenue; Beach Drive becomes the main north–south route through Rock Creek Park.) Continue straight on Beach Drive at Klingle Avenue on the left and Piney Branch Parkway on the right. There is a traffic light at Beach Drive and Park Road/Tilden Street. In 0.3 mile past this, bear left at an intersection with Blagden Avenue. One hundred yards past this, turn left off Beach Drive onto Broad Branch Road. (*Note:* Beach Drive from this point north to Military Road is closed on weekends and holidays.) Cross Rock Creek and immediately turn right on Glover Road, following signs for the Rock Creek Nature Center. In less than a mile, fork left and uphill, avoiding Ross Drive, which forks right and downhill. In 0.8 mile past this fork, turn right into the nature center parking area.

From downtown Washington, D.C.: Follow directions above from the intersection of the Rock Creek and Potomac Parkway and Virginia Avenue. Or, take New Hampshire Avenue north from DuPont Circle for 0.6 mile. Turn left onto 16th Street NW and, in 3 miles, turn right onto an entrance ramp for Military Road. In 1 mile, turn left onto Glover Road. In 0.5 mile, turn left into the nature center parking area.

From Maryland and I-495 (Capital Beltway): Take exit 31B / Georgia Avenue, following signs for Georgia Avenue South and Silver Spring. Once on Georgia Avenue, stay in either of the two right lanes so that, in 0.3 mile from I-495, you can exit right onto 16th Street. In 3.1 miles, turn right and merge onto Military Road. In 1 mile, turn left onto Glover Road. In 0.5 mile, turn left into the nature center parking area. Trailhead GPS: N38 57.594' / W77 03.103'

THE HIKE

Rock Creek Park, at its broadest, is only a mile wide. It is a nearly 10-mile-long narrow stream valley park that passes in this Google Earth age as the long green swath of trees separating downtown Washington, D.C., and Georgetown. But to look at it as a single homogenous unit is to miss the small details that make moving between the upland woods and the streamside floodplains a joy.

Unmarked, but well used, are several fishermen's paths through floodplains along Rock Creek. If you're hiking the Valley Trail, you'll find one in a wide bend in the river north of Riley Spring Bridge; the other is between West Beach Drive and Boundary Bridge. They are the proverbial low road, alternatives to the higher, drier route of the official Valley Trail.

One advantage in following them is personal satisfaction. These unmarked paths bring you close to the creek. On a sandbar, a few tree logs that washed downstream in a long-ago high flood sit high and dry, perfect perches for a snack and relaxing. The stream is a melodious riffle, not so loud that you can't hear bird chatter. A hiker told us that come autumn, there's a hint of Monet in the air. Rock Creek in calm water reflects back yellow and red leaves on overhanging trees, making a shimmering mirage of color.

In terms of plants, the floodplain just feels different from the upland. Here, there is more smooth alder but less holly, which is abundant in the understory of the drier forests that cover the stream valley's sloping hills. There is American horn-

The park's namesake: "Rock Creek"

beam, a skinny tree whose rippling trunk and tight gray bark give the appearance of muscles. It's an apt comparison; this tough, heavy wood was preferred for making the handles of axes and sledgehammers. Yellow poplar and American beech are two of the main trees you'll find in an upland forest, but in the floodplain, they're replaced by eastern black walnut. Donald Culross Peatttie, in his book *A Natural History of Trees,* ranks black walnut second only behind pecan in usefulness. The nontimber forest product program at Virginia Tech lists a number of uses for the tree: Indians chewed the bark to ease toothaches, and processed eastern black walnut shells are "soft grit abrasives" perfect for "cleaning jet engines, electronic circuit boards, ships, and automobile gear systems."

The northern section of Rock Creek Park is the perfect spot to "converse" with both the upland woods and streamside floodplains. A long stretch of Western Ridge Trail, north from Bingham Drive to Beach Drive, covers hilly terrain. It is the largest chunk of unspoiled woodland in the park, with only Wise Road bisecting it. This is the territory of the great horned owl and the screech owl.

A detour from this heavy upland forest down along Pinehurst Branch leads to other discoveries. By October, hackberry trees are in fruit along the Pinehurst Branch Trail, offering songbirds, like the cedar waxwing, valuable fuel. There are three shallow-water fords across the branch on our route; the last is a scramble up the stream bank to dry ground. The trail uphill is a narrow path that in summer almost disappears beneath the crowded shrub understory. In no time, you're standing atop a knoll amid red oak and tulip poplar. In this spot, in a park that records two million recreational visits annually, you can hear an acorn drop.

MILES AND DIRECTIONS

0.0   START from the front entrance of the Rock Creek Nature Center. Follow a paved path west past the Edge of Woods Trail on the right. Where the path Ts, turn right (north) onto the green-blazed Western Ridge Trail, which here shares the route with a paved bike path. A small sign at this junction points the way to Fort DeRussy, which is also to the right. Walk downhill to four-lane Military Road and cross straight over.

KID APPEAL

Check out the cool live beehive at the nature center. You can watch honeybees at work safely behind glass. It's connected to the outdoors through a plastic tube so the bees can leave to collect their pollen. Watch them do the "waggle" dance, a signal to others in the hive when they have found a new source of nectar. The activity of these highly social, busy bees ensures there will be wildflowers along park trails each spring.

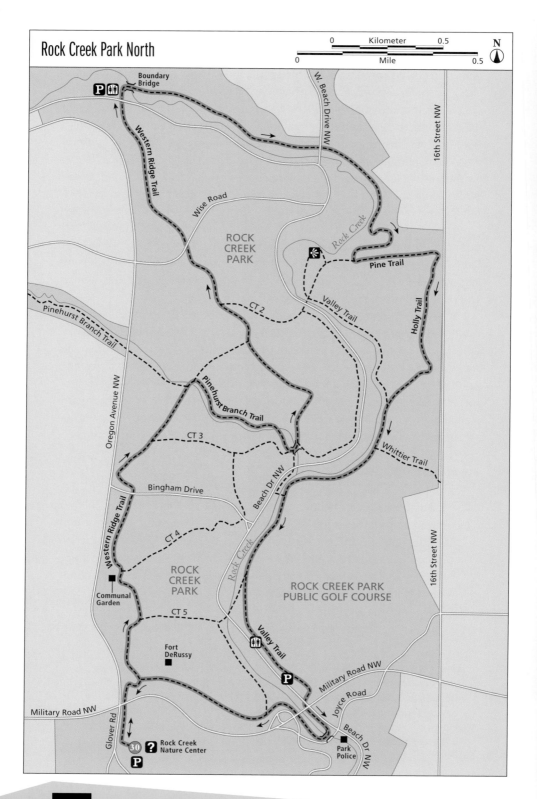

0   Kilometer   0.5

0   Mile   0.5

N

Boundary
Bridge

P

W. Beach Drive NW

16th Street NW

Western Ridge Trail

Wise Road

Rock Creek

ROCK
CREEK
PARK

Pine Trail

CT 2

Valley Trail

Holly Trail

Pinehurst Branch Trail

Pinehurst Branch Trail

CT 3

Whittier Trail

Oregon Avenue NW

Bingham Drive

Beach Dr NW

CT 4

Western Ridge Trail

Rock Creek

ROCK
CREEK
PARK

ROCK CREEK PARK
PUBLIC GOLF COURSE

16th Street NW

Communal
Garden

CT 5

Valley Trail

Fort
DeRussy

P

Military Road NW

Joyce Road

Military Road NW

Glover Rd

30   ?   Rock Creek
Nature Center

P

Beach Dr NW

Park
Police

0.2   Turn right at an interpretive sign for Fort DeRussy. In the next 0.1 mile, you will veer left off the paved path as Western Ridge Trail becomes a wide dirt trail. Soon after this, make a right (north) turn at a double green blaze as Western Ridge Trail becomes a narrow woods trail. (**Side trip:** The wide dirt path that continues straight from this double green blaze is a horse trail. In 200 yards or so, it passes the ruins of Fort DeRussy, a Civil War–era defense. This is also the return leg of this hike.)

0.5   Turn left at a double green blaze for Western Ridge Trail. (**Note:** Straight ahead is Cross Trail 5 [CT 5], which descends to Millerhouse Ford on Rock Creek.)

0.6   Emerge from the woods and trace a horse pasture fence on your right. At the end of the fence line, turn right (north) and walk between the horse pasture and a community garden on the right. The trail meets a paved road. Turn left (west) on the road, keeping a line of stubby wooden posts on your right.

0.7   Turn right onto a paved path marked by a wooden post with a green blaze for Western Ridge Trail. (**Note:** This path is immediately past a gated road that will parallel the trail for a few hundred yards.)

0.9   Cross Bingham Drive diagonally left. On the far side, Western Ridge Trail is still a paved path. Within a hundred yards, follow Western Ridge Trail as it forks left. Walk another 20 feet and turn right (north) on Western Ridge, which is now a path of dirt and crushed rock.

1.1   Stay straight on green-blazed Western Ridge Trail at a junction with Cross Trail 3 (CT 3).

1.3   Western Ridge Trail veers right at a fork in the trail. Follow it a few feet downhill to a four-way trail junction. Turn right (east) onto the Pinehurst Branch Trail and descend to cross the branch at a picturesque wading pool. This trail is for foot traffic only and is one of the most scenic in the park.

1.6   Cross Pinehurst Branch again at another scenic spot. The stream, now on your left side, makes a wide bend. At low water, exposed stream rocks are a nice place to perch and soak in the scenery.

1.7   Pinehurst Branch Trail reaches a four-way trail junction. Turn left (east) and descend the stream bank and cross Pinehurst Branch. On the opposite side, turn left (north) and start to climb an unnamed, unmarked footpath.

The route is steep on a narrow footpath that in summer is nearly overrun by shrubs and small trees.

1.8 At a T junction with another unnamed, unmarked trail, turn left (west).

2.1 Turn right (north) onto the green-blazed Western Ridge Trail.

2.2 Stay straight (north) on Western Ridge Trail at a junction with Cross Trail 2 (CT 2), which heads downhill to the right to Riley Spring Bridge on Rock Creek.

2.5 Cross Wise Road and reenter the woods on Western Ridge Trail, which here is a dirt footpath.

2.9 Western Ridge Trail ends at Beach Drive. Walk straight across the road, reentering the woods at a wood trail sign that marks the trailhead for the blue-blazed Valley Trail. Briefly, this dirt footpath skirts the Boundary Bridge parking area on your left. (**Note:** There is a chemical toilet at the parking area.)

3.0 Turn right (north) and follow Valley Trail, now a wide, graded path of dirt and crushed rock, across Rock Creek on the Boundary Bridge. A few feet past the bridge, veer right (east) off Valley Trail onto a well-trod, but unmarked, fisherman's path. (**Note:** The fisherman's path and Valley Trail are near West Beach Drive. We prefer the fisherman's path—the low road, if you will—because it keeps us close to the creek and is good for sightings of birds like great blue heron.)

3.6 Merge with the Valley Trail just before a bridge on West Beach Drive. Veer right onto the blue-blazed Valley Trail and pass beneath the bridge.

4.2 Climb the Valley Trail to a junction with the yellow-blazed Pine Trail. Turn left (east) onto Pine Trail and begin climbing. (**Side trip:** At this junction, turn right instead and walk 0.1 mile to an overlook onto Rock Creek. After enjoying the view, return to Pine Trail and resume this route.)

4.4 Pine Trail levels at a junction with Holly Trail. Turn right (south) onto Holly Trail and immediately begin to descend on a narrow dirt footpath. You'll climb into and out of a seasonal stream in a steep-sided gully. (**Note:** Straight uphill on Pine Trail leads to 16th Street.)

5.0 After a steep descent on Holly Trail, reach a T junction with the blue-blazed Valley Trail. Turn left (south) onto Valley Trail. Soon after, the trail passes beneath Sherrill Drive Bridge. Keep an eye out for a blue blaze on the bridge abutment.

5.1 Stay straight (south) on Valley Trail as Whittier Trail branches left (east). For the next 1.5 miles, it is a wide, flat streamside dirt path.

5.6 *Stay alert:* Follow the Valley Trail as it veers left (southeast) and uphill as a narrow, rocky footpath. (**Note:** The streamside trail that continues straight from this junction is Cross Trail 5 [CT 5]. It crosses Rock Creek at Milkhouse Ford.)

5.8 Pass by a park service bathroom on the right side of Valley Trail.

6.0 A series of switchbacks carries the Valley Trail off the hillside and down to Beach Drive. Turn left (south) and walk along the road shoulder beneath the Military Road bridge. When you see the road shoulder getting pinched into a narrow strip of grass by the looming hillside on your left, cross Beach Road and continue south on the paved bike path.

6.2 Reach the intersection of Joyce Road and Beach Drive. Turn right (west) onto Joyce Road. Cross Rock Creek and immediately, on the other side, turn right (north) onto a paved bike path. Follow it as it passes beneath Military Road. Rock Creek is through the trees off to the right.

6.4 Turn right (north) onto an unnamed horse trail that crosses the bike path. Walk a few feet to where the horse trail forks. Here, bear left and begin an

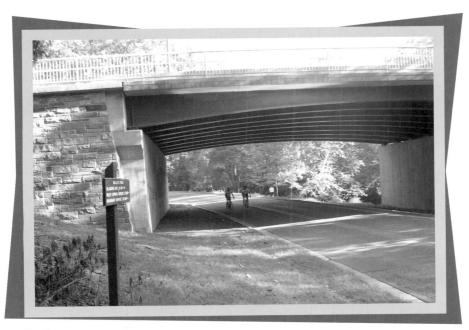

Bicyclists

uphill climb. (**Note:** The right fork of the trail goes north alongside Rock Creek to CT 5 and eventually Milkhouse Ford.)

6.8 Pass the spur trail to Fort DeRussy on the right. Within 200 yards, merge onto the green-blazed Western Ridge Trail by continuing to walk straight on the dirt trail. Avoid the green-blazed leg of Western Ridge Trail that heads right (north) at this merge. After a walking a few hundred feet more, veer right onto a paved bike path, which shares the route with Western Ridge Trail.

6.9 Turn left (south) on the combined bike path/Western Ridge Trail. Walk downhill to Military Road and cross over. The path then climbs uphill alongside Glover Road.

7.0 Turn left at a sign for the nature center.

7.1 HIKE ENDS at the Rock Creek Nature Center.

HIKE INFORMATION

Local information: Destination DC, Washington, D.C.; (202) 789-7000; www.washington.org

Local events/attractions: The Carter Barron Amphitheatre, Rock Creek Park, Washington, D.C.; (202) 426-0486; www.nps.gov/rocr/planyourvisit/cbarron.htm. Hosts summer entertainment from Shakespeare to jazz and reggae music.

Good eats: The Parkway Deli, Rock Creek Shopping Center, Grubb Road, Silver Spring, MD; (301) 587-2675; www.theparkwaydeli.com

Red Dog Cafe, Rock Creek Park Shopping Center, Grubb Road, Silver Spring, MD; (301) 588-6300; www.reddogcafe.com

Local outdoor stores: Hudson Trail Outfitters, 4530 Wisconsin Ave. NW, Washington, D.C.; (202) 363-9810; www.hudsontrail.com

Hike tours: Ranger-led horseback tours are offered in the park. There are also a host of ranger and Junior Ranger programs led from the nature center.

Organizations: Potomac Appalachian Trail Club (PATC), 118 Park St. SE, Vienna, VA; (703) 242-0315; www.potomacappalachian.org. Maintains the Valley Trail, Western Ridge Trail, and the connecting trails.

> 🌿 **Green Tip:**
> *Printing out hike directions or a map at home uses less carbon than it takes to ship the map and drive yourself to a store.*

Hike Index

About the Authors

Bill and Mary Burnham have successfully blended their love of the outdoors with backgrounds in journalism and photography for more than fifteen years. For their first book they spent two full years hiking and writing about the best trails in the Old Dominion. The result, *Hiking Virginia*, a FalconGuide, received a National Outdoor Book Award. *The Florida Keys Paddling Atlas* also earned a NOBA as the best guidebook of 2008. Among their nine books are two in Globe Pequot Press's how-to Knack series: *Car Camping for Everyone* and *Kayaking*. They live on the Eastern Shore of Virginia, where they guide kayak trips, write for several publications, and post their adventures on www.burnhamvirginia.com and www.burnham-florida.com.